Suck Less at Life

Defy Mediocrity & Live without Regrets

Cyndi Lewis

Copyright © 2024 by Cyndi Lewis

No part of this book may be used or reproduced in any manner without written permission from the publisher.

First edition 2024

Cover Photography: Bailey Jo Tardy

(www.baileyjophotographymn.com)

For the love of my life, Andrew. Thank you for giving up your anonymity to support my dreams and for putting up with me when I stress out because of putting too much unnecessary pressure on myself. I could not have risen to these heights without the strength of your love to ground me. I love you, always.

For the friends and family in my life who have encouraged and supported me, thank you for letting me be part of your worlds, and thank you for standing beside me under my umbrella of life.

A very special thank you to my silent partner, who believed in me more than anyone else… I couldn't have gotten here without you.

Contents

Introduction i

Chapter 1: Making Adulty Friends 1

Chapter 2: Be the Life of Your Parties 25

Chapter 3: How to Make Time Your B*tch 45

Chapter 4: Beware of the Green-Eyed FOMO Monster 77

Chapter 5: Bullies, They Aren't Just for Kids 95

Chapter 6: Stress is Stressful 121

Chapter 7: Go for the Gold Medal in Healthy Living 141

Chapter 8: "Sweatpants" Is My Safe Word 161

Chapter 9: Girl Math Won't Help You Retire Early 177

Chapter 10: Meal Planning for Those Who Hate the Grocery Store 199

Chapter 11: I Have a Selfie Stick, and I'm Not Afraid to Use It! 213

Chapter 12: No More I Love You's 231

Chapter 13: Don't Be a Lemming, Be a Leader......243

Chapter 14: It's Not Failure If You Learn from It..259

Chapter 15: Be a Good Human..............................275

Chapter 16: Happiness Is a Choice........................287

Chapter 17: Live without Regrets..........................299

Bonus Chapter: Suck Less At Sex..........................305

Introduction

My life's motto is, "If everyone sucked less, the world would be such a better place," which has been the inspiration for The Suck Less Series. This third installment in the series is more of an overarching prequel to the broad topic of sucking less… at everything and striving to achieve goals while living without regrets.

Everyone's unique journey through life is shaped by family, upbringing, environment, experiences, and choices made that are good and bad. All these factors are what drive us to make the decisions that we do all day, every day. However, unless we are exposed to different perspectives and experiences, we are not likely to change our behaviors to deviate too far from what we know and the places we operate from to feel safe.

The older I get, and the more experiences I have, the more I realize that I want to live my life without regrets. I'm a doer, not a sayer, and as someone who takes every idea and runs with it, I know that I will be able to say that I have lived my life to its fullest when my time ends.

In striving to be the best in everything I do, I always end up realizing that I still need to put effort into sucking less. No matter how much I want to function at my peak performance 100% of the time, more often than I'd like to admit, I need to be reminded to take my own advice, and it's humbling. Keep in mind that as I try to help you, I'm also actively trying to suck less right beside you.

The first step to working on sucking less at life is finding your internal motivation. When I share that I'm indulging in a new passion, many people express, "I'd love to do that," or "I've started that." My response is always the same. "Stop talking about it and do it." We don't come to the end of our lives and think, "I wish I had tried fewer things." That'd be dumb. Yes, you will try many things, and some endeavors you will fail at, some you will be okay at, and some you will kick ass at. The important thing is that you need to do and try these new things. Being of a learning mindset will propel you forward as you seek to conquer new and more difficult challenges.

Don't get me wrong, I'm fully aware that life is hard, exhausting, and stressful, but excuses will always be excuses. The fact of the matter is that people will always make time for the things they find important, and it's time that you start assessing your priorities because none of us knows how long we will have to live our lives to the fullest and to be the best versions of ourselves that we can be.

With the advice in this book, I hope that you will be inspired to suck a little less at a minimum of one topic because while part of the reason I write these books is to push myself to be a doer and not a sayer, ultimately, I just want to help and inspire others to make positive changes and find more happiness in their lives.

This book is meant to help you think about the different aspects and opportunities of life and how you can work to improve your life, find happiness, and suck a little bit less.

In the way that you've grown to appreciate, this book offers dueling perspectives. My loving and reluctant husband has donated his unfiltered advice in the latter half of each chapter in a She Said, He Said format. And yes, our fictitious and lovable friends, Dick and Jane, will be present and happy to be learning alongside us about how to suck less at life, defy mediocrity, and live without regrets.

Backstory note so you're not lost later: My second husband, Andrew, is a police officer in a city two hours away from where I live. We met later in life and had separate lives, so he will be living over two hours away until he retires two-and-a-half years from now (April 2024) and moves in with me and my two boys from my first marriage (ages 9 and 12) Andrew has an adult daughter who is 23.

Chapter 1:

Making Adulty Friends

SHE SAID

If you think finding your soulmate is hard, trying to find a new bestie as an adult is right up there too in terms of difficulty level. Making friends as an adult is not as simple or easy as making friends on the playground in kindergarten. You can't just walk up to a group of gal pals at a restaurant and ask, "Can I play with you?" Well, I guess you could try. Let me know how that goes. You never know; it could be a fun social experiment that I would totally tune in to watch.

Being without a friend support system can be very lonely, especially if you are also without a life partner. While I have been very fortunate to have family, friends, and partners, I have witnessed many who struggle to make genuine connections, and I'm here to help if you find yourself in that camp.

Why do so many adults struggle to make friends later in life? There are lots of reasons, and here are a few:

1. Many adults have already filled their friend roster and are not looking to add any new members.
2. Some adults have bred a small sports team and don't have enough time, energy, or clean laundry for new friends.
3. Some people are introverts and prefer to spend their free time alone.
4. You live in a small town, everyone knows everyone, and no one has time for you: a new person.

We all need social interaction with friends that we can laugh with and share experiences with outside of our family obligations, but how can we make new friends when so many others aren't in the market for another friend? Let's attack these issues like salespeople who need to learn how to break through barriers to sales. After all, you are selling your awesomeness to others for a mutual benefit.

Issue #1: Sorry, My Friend Roster is Full

When I moved to Duluth, MN, I was going nuts in my home without any local friends. I had made quite a network in the Twin Cities where we moved from, but alas, we moved north in the summer when most people were the busiest. School was out, so I couldn't friend-attack people there. What to do?

An extrovert at heart, I came up with a plan. I would talk to everyone that I met, and I'd go from there. And so, the friend attacks commenced: I talked the ears off waitstaff at restaurants, tellers at the bank, and clerks at the grocery store. You name the errand, and I tried to make friends in that situation. Every pleasant interaction was followed up by, "Are you on Facebook? We should be friends." Yes, I'm old. I use Facebook to connect with people in my personal life.

Making a genuine connection with someone when you meet will rely on your intuition. You can usually read people and gauge their level of interest if you ask for their contact information upfront. If you reach out a few times to make plans, and you don't get a favorable response, then that person was just being polite to you in person. However, you will meet people with whom you connect in the strangest of places, and sometimes they can turn out to be your closest friends. If yours truly can make a friend during an OBGYN appointment when the practitioner is up her hoo-ha, you can make friends with strangers too.

Trying to make friends with people who may think they have enough friends isn't impossible, but it's a numbers game, just like dating. Don't give up. It only takes one for you to find a true connection, and that one friend will have been worth any and all uncomfortable situations you put yourself in whilst trying to make connections.

Issue #2: Sports Team-Breeding Parents

The more kids you have, the more you probably need a break from the kids you have unless the oldest kids have become the babysitters for the youngest. Even if you have this cyclical chain of help, parenting can be an isolating endeavor if you're not careful. I can remember hardly leaving the house for my first year of parenting because I feared a potential bad baby surprise incident.

The good news is that if you are a parent, there are a ton of great ways to connect with other parents in your town. One of the first things I did when I moved north was to ask the preschool where my youngest was attending who my son's friends were. When I got the shortlist, I went home, got out some pretty blank cards, and wrote handwritten invitations to the parents of my son's friends:

"Dear (child's name)'s parents,

My son is friends with your son at preschool. Would you be interested in getting together for a play date at our house? Please let me know. My cell phone number is 555-555-5555."

People LOVE handwritten notes because getting them is so rare. Taking the time to put that kind of effort in shows someone that you are genuinely interested in making a connection, and offering to host the first meeting takes any pressure off the new family to plan or host a get-together. Using this targeted strategy, I made some great play date friends, and so can you!

When school started in the fall after we moved, I joined the Parent Teacher Organization so that I could meet other parents… and volunteer and find out more about the school my children would be attending for years. Some of my very best friends are still on the PTO board with me years later, and I cherish their friendships. However, we do tend to talk too much about PTO business when we are at parties with other non-PTO parents!

Parent friends are great for so many reasons. The ones who have a lot of children make great friends to do adulty things together with because they are usually desperately seeking sanctuary somewhere, anywhere, away from their families. I remember when my youngest was little and was following me around saying, "Mommy, mommy, mommy, mommy…"

"WHAT!?" I screamed as I whipped around.

"Meow," he said before running away happily.

Kids. And that's why you need to put some effort into finding other parent friends who are as eager as you are to seek refuge in adults-only land… the land of peace, intelligent conversation, and NOT having to hear your name playing over and over on repeat.

Of course we as parents love our children, but sometimes in order to be a healthy, happy parent, you need a break and some adult time. Don't feel bad about taking the time for yourself to spend with your new friends because you are recharging your parenting batteries and hopefully learning some great tips and tricks too.

Issue #3 Introverts Are Like Easter Eggs… with Fun Prizes Hiding Inside

I love me some introverted friends. Why? Because I talk… a lot… like pretty much all the time. Introverts are great listeners and very loyal friends. When an introvert spends time with others socially, it drains their energy, so they are very particular to whom they give that opportunity. My hubby is an introvert and one of the greatest listeners ever. Opposites attract, clearly.

When I went off to a college in Roseville, MN, I was what you could have called an introvert. Growing up in the same small town my whole life had pigeonholed me into the personality I started with, not allowing me to evolve into the person I wanted to be. "When I go to college, I'm going to reinvent myself!" I thought. If you've been following my book series, you probably know by now that when I decide to do something, it's best just to get out of my way and let me do it. That part of my personality has NOT changed over time.

The first week of school, I walked up to many a stranger and introduced myself. There was one girl in particular whose meeting I remember vividly. She stood awkwardly alone out in the green space in front of the main building, the sun lighting her red hair into a fiery blaze.

"Hi! I'm Cyndi. What's your name, and where are you from?" I blurted out as I inserted myself into her bubble of quiet. She was the most introverted person I think that I've ever met, but we became the closest of friends very quickly. Sharing many mugs full of Goldfish crackers and lime Kool-Aid, we attempted to solve the mystery that was flirting and how to get boyfriends. Ironic, isn't it, that I've gone from not knowing how to flirt to advising about love and relationships. Life's funny like that.

One of my good friends in Duluth is an introvert, and whenever she attends one of my parties, she says, "This is the only time I ever leave the house to do anything fun... Cyndi's parties." She's great. I love how she gets a new outfit for all my themed parties with dress codes. Because I know she's an introvert, sometimes I plan to do fun things just the two of us because that's when introverts open up... in the one-on-one sessions, and you know how much I love to meddle in other people's lives. My hubby says that if I didn't meddle, I'd die.

However, if you are an introvert, my advice is a bit different. While introverts do need quite a bit of alone time to recharge and be happy, sometimes they isolate themselves too much and find themselves a bit depressed. If an extrovert approaches your introverted self, just go with it and see where it leads you. One of my good friends is an introvert. I met her when I started a new job; she hired me! One Friday morning, I found myself without plans for what was shaping up to be I-must-be-outside weather, so I invited her to join me at the beach. Years later she told me that she had wanted to say no but forced herself out of her comfort zone to go, and she's so glad she did.

Introverts love extroverted friends. They pull introverts out into the sunlight of life, and everyone is happier for it. Try to connect with an extrovert in any of the above-mentioned solutions. Oftentimes, extroverts like me cannot have enough friends and view friending introverts like Easter egg hunts. We love the hunt and the prizes we find when we crack the hard shell of an introvert open to discover an amazing person and a new friend.

Where were those extroverts to yank me out of my Easter egg when I was in middle school and high school?! Oh well, I'm leading the Easter egg hunt now. Go forth, and crack those shells… just be wary of the eggs that sat in the sun too long and are now stinky.

Issue #4: You're Not a Native, So You're an Outsider

In the first year that I lived in Duluth, I wrote an article about finding adult friendships for a local blog. When the article was published, many subscribers agreed that it was and is very difficult to make friends in a town like this, where many have lived their whole lives. They're not wrong. Most people don't share the friend-attack method that I use.

If you find yourself in a small town, one of the easiest ways to make a new friend is to become friends with a coworker… or court someone with hopes of making her your work wife. Think about the person whose office you waste the first fifteen to twenty minutes of your Monday in. That person is your potential work spouse. What turns a work spouse into a friend is taking the relationship to the next level, which is essentially seeing each other outside of the office.

> *When Dick and Jane moved to the suburbs, Jane started a new job at a marketing agency, but she felt very out of place. She didn't know anyone in town, let alone at work. She found herself drawn to Sandy because they worked on the same floor in the same department, and they seemed to be around the same age, which set them apart from some of the younger girls in the office.*
>
> *Sandy kept to herself, staying in her office most of the time, and she didn't seem to be close to anyone else in the office, which made her single and up for grabs. On Jane's fourth day of work, she was fired up about something, and she needed to vent to someone other than her husband... someone who wouldn't try to solve her problem but who would instinctively know how to listen and commiserate.*

Knocking tentatively on Sandy's open door, Jane asked, "Hey, Sandy, mind if I come in for a few minutes?"

Looking happy to be offered something more interesting than the project that she was having trouble concentrating on, Sandy said, "Sure Jane! What's up?"

"I just had to tell someone how annoyed I am at our movers! Our furniture was delayed when we moved here, and now they're saying it will be another week and a half!" Jane exploded.

"Oh, that sucks! I'm sorry," empathized Sandy. "We had an issue like that when we had bought a new couch. We sold the old one the morning when the new one was supposed to be delivered, and then the store called to tell us it hadn't come in and it would be another week. We had to sit on lawn chairs until it came!" The commiserating continued, and Jane had begun courting Sandy as her work wife.

A few months later, Dick was out of town for a bachelor party weekend, and Jane was looking for some girl time.

"Hey Sandy, what are your plans for this weekend?" She asked her friend, not knowing if Sandy wanted the friendship to extend beyond the office walls.

"I don't know yet," Sandy responded.

"Do you want to go hiking? I think the weather is supposed to be really nice," she said.

"Sure! I'd love to. Maybe we can stop at that new restaurant for lunch!"

Sandy agreed, and that weekend, Jane and Sandy consummated their work-spouse union by taking the relationship to the next level.

If you make friends with a coworker, and that coworker is a local, you just multiplied your friend circle as she will likely introduce you to others from the area. If your new work spouse isn't local, then you'll both have that in common, and that's a win too.

As I started to gather friends in my new hometown, I felt more connected to the new community I was excited to call home. Six years later, I'm still friends with many of these people I pounced on at their place of work or my place of work, and I love it. However, there have been some unfortunate happenings in my quest to hoard friends.

When I moved here, I moved into my dream house… the FOMO house. Unfortunately, when I got divorced and downsized into a home a fraction of the size of the first, I lost several friends. Could adult friends have been so superficial that they only wanted to be my friend because of the prestige of the house I lived in? The short and sad answer is yes.

The immaturity of the friend uncoupling bothered me a great deal, but with more time that passes, the more thankful I am that it happened. My life downsize revealed who my true friends were. When I could no longer give out personalized goodie bags and host in elegance, my real friends stuck around. The friends I lost who also had large homes and were all about friendships with people of the like weren't friends I would want to invest in and foster relationships with.

Friendships are a funny thing, and they change as our lives change. Sometimes we make new and unexpected friends, and sometimes we grow apart and lose touch with our best friends. When you as an adult have less and less free time and become choosy with how you spend it, friendships need to make sense and be valuable to you and your life.

In my world, a friend is a genuinely good person with whom I share at least one common interest. If we can share a good laugh and sometimes a good cry, I'll take you. I don't care what you do, what you look like, where you're from, how big your house is, or what kind of car you drive. Titles and prestige don't impress me one bit. Being a good person that's fun to be around is pretty much my vetting process for friends. However, if you don't think I'm funny, it's going nowhere.

I have this one dear friend who has since moved away, but she dropped everything one night at 9:00 pm to come take me to the ER when I was alone and had a painful UTI. Her husband dropped her off, but by the time we got back to my house after the ER and pharmacy, it was very late. She needed to get a ride home, but the only taxi service in the area couldn't pick her up until after midnight. "You go rest. I'll wait up. It'll be okay; I'm just glad you're starting to feel better," she said.

She's also the friend who came to help me pack when I was moving during my divorce. Her life with three kids was busy and complicated, but she set up a playpen in the yard for her youngest and said, "I'm here to help with whatever you need!" I miss her so much. She was and is what a friend should be: caring, nonjudgmental, and fiercely loyal to the end.

HE SAID

She: How have you made friends as an adult, and where?

He: I don't make adult friends very easily.

She: Yeah, but you've had them. Where did you make them?

He: They have just been people that I matched with personality-wise. I learn very quickly who I can and can't trust, and I'm usually drawn to those people with certain traits that are rare... like integrity and honesty...

She: Okay, but where are you meeting them?

He: Usually at work.

She: What about the guy who owned the bar?

He: That was a place where we all hung out. People used to approach with an angle because they wanted something. I don't kiss people's asses, and I'm not going to fluff you up. I'm usually quiet, and when I meet people who don't have an agenda and are real, I latch onto those people.

She: What about the tattoo guy? Were you friends with him before you started getting tattoos?

He: No. I started getting tattoos and talking to him, and we had a lot of similar interests. He was like a big fish in a small pond where people were drawn to him like coolness by association, but when someone comes along who just wants to spend time with you and likes you, those people feel safe with those kinds of people. I'm very good at reading people, and I don't push people's boundaries. I know what to say and what not to say, and I think that people value that.

She: What purpose do you feel like adult friends serve?

He: You've gotta have some people that you can talk to and trust and that will back you up and be there for you when things go down because a lot of things in life are hard. If you don't have people you can trust and that will go to bat for you, who do you have if you don't have family close by? When you don't have family close, you have to build your own family. Regardless of how introverted you might be, we are all social beings.

She: When you retire in a few years, do you think you'll want to make friends here?

He: No, but I'll want to connect with the friends that I haven't had the time to pay much attention to.

She: Okay, but if you did want to make friends here, how would you go about doing that?

He: I wouldn't try to do it, it would need to happen organically. Going out looking for friends seems odd to me.

She: That's what I did.

He: Well, you're extroverted, and you can be friends with anyone.

She: What do you find to be the characteristics you value most in an adult friend?

He: Being real, normal, and doesn't expect anything out of me. Someone with honor and integrity and who doesn't care what other people think and isn't looking to be validated. All my closest friends have been like that. People who are always excited to see you and who are always happy for what you're doing. There's no agenda. My friends only have a few close friends that they trust and want to be around.

She: Do you think that people should have friends of the opposite sex?

He: No, I don't think that works.

She: Why?

He: Because how does that look in society? People will always assume that you're doing something, especially if you're also in a relationship. Usually, regardless of your gender, when you get into a relationship, the focus shifts to the relationship, and then friends get pushed to the side. For same-sex, it's not as big of a deal because you're not usually super reliant on that person, but for opposite-sex friends, it's not going to work.

She: Have you ever had to let an adult friend go over something petty or childish?

He: I haven't, but I've seen it happen.

She: Are you talking about me?

He: No. When a man breaks off a friendship with a guy, it's usually over something big.

She: Like what?

He: Women.

She: *(Laughing)* That makes sense.

While my introverted, man-of-few-words husband always says, "You can't be everybody's friend," that doesn't mean that you shouldn't try to push yourself out of your comfort bubble to try to make new friends. That is, if you want more friends. He's not wrong in that some people will not warm to you immediately or want to be your friend at all, but so what? You do you, and there will be people that celebrate your quirks and embrace your flaws.

As you get older, and everyone's lives get filled with work, kids, family, sports, volunteering, etc., you have less and less time to spend with friends. However, the beauty of mature adult relationships is that no matter how long it has been since you saw each other last, you can pick up right where you left off with no animosity about the gap of time that had lapsed.

A real friend will be there for you and won't judge but will also call you out on your crap. Good adult friends love you, and they don't want you to become or be viewed as an ass hat, so they'll let you know when you step out of line and will expect you to do them the same courtesy.

Healthy adult relationships aren't jealous, scorekeeping, or petty. They lift you when you are down, they get mad at the same things you are mad at, they help you out when you are in crisis, they are there for you when you need it the most, and they love you for who you are and don't try to change you. When you make adult friendships like that, count yourself truly lucky and cherish them as much as you would the person you choose to be your partner for life because they are just as rare.

Chapter 2:

Be the Life of Your Parties

SHE SAID

The very first time I attempted to make a "meal" was in my college dorm room. "Meal" is in quotations because I'm not sure that what I made fits the standard definition of the word. Corn straight from the can; dry, pan-fried chicken; and minute rice served on lime green plastic plates with matching cups filled with Kool-Aid. A crowning achievement in fine dining and culinary success!

Well, my entertaining has evolved a bit since then but only because I was inspired to elevate to entertain more formally. Entertaining can take many forms, is a lot of work, and it's not something everyone aspires to be good at. I love entertaining because it's a great way for a type A+

extroverted person like me to indulge all my idiosyncrasies: decorating, cooking, being creative, organizing, bringing people together, and being the life of the party. If formal entertaining is something you're curious about, I hope you can find some inspiration and ideas from my experiences.

Every year I host four of what I call "mom parties" because they start at 4:00 pm and last until 8:00 pm... if we're lucky to still be awake by then. Most of us have kids and are tired by eight, and some of my friends need to get home to tuck their kids into bed. Each party usually takes place in the same month and has the same recurring theme as the prior year. Social media invites usually go out either right after the last party of the year or in early January because some of my friends are as bad as I am when it comes to planning out their whole lives. If I want to get on their schedules, I need to get there first, which means planning in January for a Christmas party in November.

The first rule I made up for my parties is that the dress code IS required for entry because they're my parties, and that means I get to make up the rules no matter how weird they are (remember, friends embrace your quirks!). If someone arrives wearing sweatpants, she will not be let inside the house, and sweatpants have become a running joke… or threat, rather.

I like to dress for my parties like how people used to dress for dinner. I suppose you could liken me to the eccentric old lady I knew when interning at an architecture and design firm. She wore all her dresses layered on top of each other when she went on a trip because she didn't want to check a bag. Oh, and she always had lipstick on her teeth and outside her lip line but like most eccentrics, she was beloved and a riot to be around. I'm fun and eccentric like that but with a better fashion sense and makeup that stays inside the lines of my face.

One of my favorite quirky dinner party traditions is The Boobie Cup. You heard me… boobie… like boobs, not the bird. For one of my very first dinner parties, I purchased wine glass markers that were an assortment of flower heads with suction cups on the back so they would stick to the side of wine glasses. I was in the kitchen, and I looked across the room to the table I had elaborately set, and the wine marker that was supposed to look like a sunflower (yellow outside, brown circular inside) looked an awful lot like part of the female reproductive anatomy.

"I can't put that one out there!" I exclaimed in a panic to my friend, who had come early to help set up. "It looks like a boob!" We decided to see if others thought so, and they agreed. I had the very best idea at that party: whoever came late or arrived last to the party would have to drink from The Boobie Cup of Shame. In tiny little back letters, I wrote, "I will not be late" around the circumference of the boobie flower, and the legend of The Boobie Cup was born!

It became a party tradition and a running joke that was embraced immediately. Friends would text ahead of time, "Just give me The Boobie Cup because I'm running late." One of my friends had the date of a party wrong and missed it entirely, and she followed up with, "I'll take The Boobie Cup at the next party since I screwed up the date so badly."

At each party, The Boobie Cup recipient must ceremoniously get her photo taken with the cup at the party. When my very good friend moved away, I gave her the original "Boobie" to carry on the entertaining tradition in her new town... in the way of the sisterhood of the traveling Boobie Cup.

That gesture, however, left me without a boobie... what was a hostess to do? I bought a cheap wine glass at the dollar store (back when things cost one dollar) and paint markers, and I painted a large replica on the side of the glass with the same words written in a circle around the areola: "I will not be late". And for added dramatic effect, on the opposite side of the glass, I wrote: "I'm sorry I suck!" Every person who claimed The Boobie Cup of Shame had her name and the date written on the cup, and there is a new cup for every year like a trophy. It's one of my favorite traditions, and my friends just go with it because sometimes we want to be silly and share a good laugh.

Coming full circle, as I was painting this year's wine glass with the ceremonial boobie icon, my youngest son observantly said, "That looks like a flower." "Yes, that's *exactly* what it is... a flower..." They don't get sarcasm yet, bless their little naive hearts.

If you're inspired to start a mom dinner party club, I highly recommend it. Here's an overview of my party circuit for guidance. We take summers off because everyone is too busy, but if I want to see a friend in the summer, we make separate one-on-one plans for lunch or dinner during the week.

Party #1: Galentine's Party or Birthday Party

Month: February *(my birthday month)*

Dress Code: Red or pink.

Décor: Red, pink, and sometimes gold décor that hangs over the dining space. Heart and OXOX glittery décor draped behind the dining table.

Party #2: Spring Party

Month: April

Dress Code: Pastels or floral prints.

Décor: Pastel floral runner and matching cloth napkins. Spring-scented floral candles, and fresh flowers.

Party #3: Burn Therapy Party

Month: September

Dress Code: Plaid, reds, browns, or oranges *(jeans acceptable only because we will be outside by the firepit and potentially handling sharp objects while consuming alcohol).*

Décor: Fall-colored cloth napkins, pumpkins, fake fall leaves, and a dark green table runner adorn the table.

Special Note: This party used to be fall-themed, but it has shifted to be the one casual party where everyone gets to bring an item of their significant other's that annoys them *(or a photo of it if it's too large or toxic to burn)*. Once someone has told her story about why the item annoys her, she tosses it into the fire, and we cheer as we watch it burn.

I thoroughly enjoyed watching my friend Hulk-style tear her husband's old underwear before she tossed it into the fire. Hilarious. Since this party is "therapeutic", we also indulge in throwing sharp objects (throwing stars, axes, and knives at the throwing wall my warrior husband made) before we turn civilized again and head indoors to eat with cloth napkins.

Party #4: Annual Christmas Party

Month: November *(Good luck scheduling anything on a weekend in December with work holiday parties, family gatherings, and the actual holiday)*

Dress Code: Sparkle, red, or green.

Décor: All that glitters, white snowflakes, ornaments, all the wonderful Christmas things.

I can still remember the first adult dinner party I was invited to. It occurred early in my first marriage, which puts me in my mid-twenties, I believe, but I still recall walking into the well-decorated, large home with awe. When I laid eyes on the matching dinner place settings and the elaborate nature of the dessert, I thought, "I want to be able to entertain like this someday."

Not everyone aspires to be the "Hostess with the Mostess", but it can have its benefits. In the throwaway society we find ourselves in, formal entertaining seems to be inching toward a permanent place in the "lost art" folder. So why entertain? It seems like a lot of work. Can't we just meet friends for dinner at a restaurant? Because it's fun, people enjoy home-cooked meals, and you don't get dirty stares from wait staff if you've been sitting together for more than an hour.

After all the furniture finally arrived at their new home, Jane was anxious to make more friends in town, so she decided to host a dinner party. She and Sandy talked about who from the office to invite, and they decided to keep it small to start with—six people total. "I have just enough place settings for six so I'm good there," Jane said as she planned out loud.

"How about I bring some fresh flowers for the table and come early to help you set up," offered Sandy.

As her potential new friends arrived, she greeted each one and offered them a drink. Appetizers were shared while they awaited dinner to be ready and for all the guests to arrive. Being her first time entertaining a group of people she didn't know very well, Jane had purchased a party conversation starter game. When the conversation lulled, she pulled out another card, and the conversation quickly started back up again with laughter and stories.

At the end of the evening, each party guest left with rosy cheeks and a smile, and as Jane and

Sandy cleaned up, they both thought it was a great success to have made new friends and to have started something new that they enjoyed.

While you are certainly welcome to do you when it comes to entertaining your way, if you want to delve into formal entertaining, here's a good place to start:

What are the things I need to be a good dinner party hostess?

1. A matching set of dinnerware, flatware, chargers, and stemware for twelve *(you do not want to have to try to expand your set after they discontinue making it)*.
2. Matching bowls and platters to serve and display food.
3. A proper expandable dining room table and chairs *(try to avoid folding chairs and tables unless it's a child's birthday party)*.
4. Centerpiece design *(often including a table runner, flowers, candles, and accouterment to match the theme or time of year)*.
5. A speaker to play soft, ambient music *(My friends give me crap for always playing the*

Yacht Rock station during my parties because the station name is so goofy).
6. Wine markers *(optional)*
7. Cloth napkins *(optional)*. If you must use disposable napkins, use the elegant white dinner napkins and not the decorative ones with the waxy surface that is completely nonfunctional as an actual napkin but works great if you want to smear food all over your face.
8. Charger plates *(optional)*

Skills to learn:

1. Napkin folding
2. How to set a formal dinner place setting
3. How to decorate a table for a dinner party

When I was inducting a new friend into my dinner party crew, she came over early to help set up. I asked her if she would put the chargers on the table, but a few moments later, I looked over at her, and she still had the first one in her hand and was turning it over and over while looking very confused. "What are you doing?" I asked her.

"I'm looking for the place to plug my phone in. You said it was a charger." Yes, I supposed that could be confusing, and we shared a good laugh over it.

"I grew up on a farm, lady!" She jested as we continued to set up.

Regardless of how many matching place settings you have, the most important thing you need to do when it comes to entertaining is to be a good hostess. That means you put yourself in a place at the table that allows you to come and go easily because it's your job to make sure everyone's glass is full, and that seconds and thirds are offered and served. As the hostess, you are also responsible for all the cleanup. Guests are guests; however, most people will offer to help or will just start helping. You can either choose to accept that help or say, "I appreciate the offer, but go enjoy yourself, you are my guest. I'll clean up." Do not assume that others will help, and if they don't, try to stay in the conversation while also cleaning up.

The hardest part of hosting is making sure that the conversation is always flowing and that everyone feels heard, special, and happy they came. My parties have gotten much smaller and have become an intimate core group of friends that doesn't need this level of maintenance anymore. If, however, you are just starting or are inviting a new person, it is your job as hostess to make sure that new person is introduced, asked questions, and given a little extra attention. All guests should leave excited to come back for your next event.

HE SAID

She: What comes to your mind when you hear "adult entertaining"?

He: Entertaining or entertainment?

She: Entertaining.

He: I don't understand. It doesn't make sense.

She: Like dinner parties, but you were supposed to come up with that on your own.

He: Adult entertaining…

She: Like entertaining as an adult!

He: That's not something I've ever been into.

She: But what would come to your mind if someone said that?

He: *(Repeating the same phrase over with increasing confusion)* Adult entertaining…

She: Like when I have people over, and I put all the stuff out, and that stuff. You got nothin'?

He: Yeah, that's not something I'm involved in.

She: Yes, you are!

He: I've never thought about it…

She: But you're a part of it every Thanksgiving. That's entertaining when you have that many people over, you organize everything, and you put all the matching stuff out. That's what I'm talking about.

He: I don't understand what you're asking. I think it's a pain in the ass!

She: *(Laughing)* What role do you think that entertaining should have in adulting?

He: It's just not important to me. I don't think it has any role.

She: Yeah, but you go to the family gatherings…

He: But that's different. It's family.

She: That's also a form of entertaining.

He: It's just a convenient opportunity to spend time with people that you don't get to see often. I think it takes a lot of work and money, but when I was a kid, we didn't have a lot of money but would get together with family for casual meals. It builds a stronger bond with people.

She: I'm talking about formal entertaining. You don't see any value in that?

He: No, that means nothing to me.

She: Who should have this skill, and at what age should they have it? I'm talking about elegant entertaining.

He: That's something that's only important if you find it important.

She: So, you think there's no place for it in normal adulting?

He: I think if you want to solidify your position in a community, it's very important. Most people are too exhausted at the end of the work week to even do that stuff.

She: Hmm... Not how I thought this conversation would go.

Being able to formally entertain as an adult is like earning extra credit. No, not everyone is cut out to do it or wants to do it, but if you push yourself to do something, be great at it. I had aspired to entertain when I was introduced to it, and I hope that my entertaining gives you some inspiration and guidelines if that's something you are excited to do.

The purpose of entertaining as an adult can be multifaceted. You can set yourself up to entertain the family that's in town, you can be the place of gathering, or you can make up your own rules and invite your friends over for a good time.

While I enjoy the dress codes for my parties, it's certainly not something that you need to incorporate. One of my less glitzy friends said to me at one of my events, "I value our friendship. You inspire me to elevate my style." That's part of the reason for my formalities... to inspire, to elevate, and to have a reason to dust off the heels and the dresses from the back of the closet and let them bring sparkle back into your life.

Even though my preference is to entertain formally because I'm psycho like that, I reluctantly agree with my husband that the real value in entertaining is held in the people that you invest the time and effort in. If that means paper plates and plastic utensils, I suppose that's all right if you still abide by the rule about what makes a good host: making sure that every guest feels special, has a great time, and leaves with a full belly.

Chapter 3:

How to Make Time Your B*tch

SHE SAID

Are there ever enough hours in the day to accomplish everything you want to achieve? Yes, there absolutely can be! If you can get a black belt in time management, you can make time your b*tch. (You cannot fathom how frustrated the grammar app got at this phrasing… it kept trying to change it to "How to Make Time for Your B*tch"! Sorry grammar app, I AM trying to use the offensive phrasing that is this chapter's namesake.)

Time management is a skill that I have been honing for my entire life. I assume that part of the reason I've become great at it is my personality's combination of anxiety mixed with perfectionism and sprinkled with control freak. Regardless of how I mutated into the time-harnessing guru I am, I am happy to be helping you take control of the limited hours you have in your day.

If you're struggling to get everything done and are stressing out, the good news is that there are time hacks you can implement to get more done than you ever have before. Learn, follow, and master these steps to suck less at time management:

Step #1: Know Your Brain Cycle

The first step in great time management is knowing when your brain works its best. I'm a morning person so I start my day early. About ten minutes after I wake up at 4:00 am, my brain starts going into hyperdrive but unfortunately, my peak brain time overlaps with my treadmill time. Even though I'm stuck on a machine, I use that time to strategically plan out my day in blocks of overlapping tasks on the timeline I start forming in my head. So many of my great ideas have happened on a treadmill, and I know that if

I don't capture those ideas at the moment, I'll lose them. When inspiration hits while I'm running, I dictate an email to myself to be logged correctly later in the day when I'm sitting at a computer.

After my workout and after I finish getting ready, then it's gray-matter task time. Writing grants, designing marketing materials, prepping for meetings, etc. are things I take care of first thing in the morning when I get to work. I typically plan to accomplish all my heavy brain usage activities before lunch if possible. If not, then I enlist the help of an energy drink.

Afternoons at work or home are for menial tasks like cleaning, cooking, data entry, addressing thank you cards, etc. If you are an evening or afternoon person, you need to allocate your tasks to suit your best brain time of the day. After you figure out when you work best and can allocate tasks accordingly, then you are ready to move on to the next step.

Step #2: Prioritize

Unfortunately, people who struggle to prioritize usually suffer more chaotic lives. Knowing how to prioritize isn't something that comes easily to some, but there are ways to learn and hone this skill. While you're making your mental plan for the day (or literal plan on paper—I fully encourage you to timeline your tasks), start to prioritize what needs doing and by when, and move those high-priority tasks to the front of either your peak brain time or peak menial work time.

Let's say that at work, I have a grant with a fast-approaching deadline, fifteen donor letters to get out before the end of the week, meetings to schedule for the following week, data entry to log, and an event planning meeting to prepare for.

The first task to prioritize and get moved to the number one peak brain timeslot is finishing the grant because it's a hard deadline and an important project. When I need a brain break, I will call to schedule meetings before people's calendars fill up. As my brain starts to fizzle out after lunch, I print the donor letters and start handwriting the addresses and personal notes because those are repetitious actions. I'll often put on lyric-less music (like elevator music) to help me focus. The next day, I will prioritize finalizing the grant first thing, and then prep my notes for the event planning meeting that I will be running. Toward the end of the week, my time frees up, and I can use the whole workday to finish up all tasks.

When I feel like my work or personal plate is overflowing and becoming overwhelming, I sit down and make lists so that I can make sure not to miss anything. The thought of forgetting or missing a deadline stresses me out. Those lists will often have high-priority items highlighted in color, and deadlines will be added when the lists get too long. Once I can look at all my tasks in one place, I always feel less overwhelmed because I can see and follow the plan to get everything accomplished. Furthermore, I find that physically crossing something off a to-do list is very satisfying.

Step #3: Delegate

If you have others in the house or at work who can assist you in accomplishing your tasks, do not be afraid to delegate. When I got backlogged at work with donor thank-you letters, I couldn't keep up and was getting overwhelmed. One of my coworkers who had fewer pressing tasks volunteered to help when she heard me having a freakout. "I'd be happy to help – just let me know when you need me," she said graciously. We worked in tandem as I made the letters, signed them, and wrote a note on them while she hand-addressed and sealed them. Done and done.

As the President of the Parent Teacher Organization, I usually try to see if someone is willing to take on a task before volunteering. Oftentimes, people who are volunteering for the organization already will happily raise their hands to lead a project if it's something they have a skillset for, you just need to wait a few moments in silence for everyone to think it over.

At home, I delegate tasks to my children in the form of daily chores or "other duties as assigned". I utilize their help at dinner by having them set the table, pour beverages, and help with the cooking according to their skill sets. They also have daily chores, which include vacuuming, cleaning the litterbox, making their beds, putting their laundry away, and emptying and loading the dishwasher. NO RULE says that because you're an adult or a parent, YOU have to do EVERYTHING. So don't, or you'll resent everyone around you and turn into a B witch.

Step #4: Multitask and Layer Activities

The most important aspect of making time your b*tch is layering time by multitasking. If you put everything that you need to accomplish down on paper as a bar on a timeline, and then overlap the things that could be done simultaneously, you will see how accomplishing everything can be done. Many times, we have pockets of time where our brains are idle while our bodies are doing something. Those are the easiest multitask overlays, like if it's your mom's birthday, so you make a point to call her on your way to work. One of the best things about overlapping phone calls with drive time is that if it's someone you don't want to spend all day talking to, you always have the "It was so great talking to you, but I just got to where I was going so I need to go" excuse. Not that anyone would ever need to use that excuse…

As I mentioned before, I multitask in the morning as I'm exercising on the treadmill. I use the cooldown time to work on my social media marketing, watch self-help videos on YouTube about how to prepare better for interviews, or dictate ideas for book chapters into my phone in the form of an email. It's very difficult to multitask on my phone when I'm running and sweating on it, but it's not impossible.

Train your brain to be able to do more than one thing at a time. Triple tasking is where I max out, but being able to do at least two things at once puts you ahead of the time management game. Things that can be triple-tasked are things that you start, walk away from, and can come back to, like dinner in the oven or laundry in the machine.

For these items, you set a completion time alarm and use the time between to engage in a task that you can finish in that period. Laundry + dinner + gardening + talking… that's quadruple tasking. Just try not to put weeds in the dryer or your phone in the oven. Don't multitask while distracted like I did once when I put my cell phone in the washing machine and didn't realize it until it was too late.

Step #5: Use Effective Tools

The very best tool that I use to make time my b*tch is my Google calendar. I remember back in college and high school when I used a paper planner because that was the only option. UGH. The lines were so small, and the writing and erasing and rewriting… so inefficient. When I made the transition from paper to a digital calendar, my life leveled up significantly.

I put EVERYTHING in my Google calendar: birthdays are PURPLE, important non-recurring items are in RED, boring reminders that aren't worth the extra effort of manually changing the color are in the default color of MAUVE, anything food-related including dining out is in GREEN, anything husband-related is YELLOW, work items are GRAY, routine maintenance items like getting my hair dyed or doing my nails are BLUE, and my trash and recycling schedule days are in ORANGE.

Another benefit to going digital is that you can share events with others. When the school calendar comes out, I put all the NO SCHOOL days into my calendar and invite my ex-husband to those "events" so that we both know when the kids don't have school. However, I may have gone a little bit extreme with my calendar when I entered my husband's work schedule up until he retires. He's got a rotating shift schedule that's something like 5 on, 3 off, 5 on, 3 off, 5 on, 4 off, 4 on, 4 off, 4 on... so planning anything was annoying until I entered five years' worth of data into my calendar. Doing that work made planning things years out a cinch... important things like the wedding he thought was premature. Oh, husband. Why do you fight me? Your efforts are futile.

I love that I can glance at my digital calendar on my phone, on my computer, anywhere, and know just by the colors what's happening all week. I love it so much, and yes, husband, I would marry it if I could. Some people still like paper organizers, and for the life of me, I cannot understand why. They can get lost, you can't schedule recurring items like birthdays, trash days, etc. It makes no sense to me. People with paper calendars seem to be the least organized people I know. Just skip it and go digital with your calendar; you'll thank me. It will remind you of things ahead of time too, which is how I have birthdays set up: a notification and an email two weeks before, a notification and an email a week before, and a notification and an email the morning of. I don't forget anything. Ever.

Step #6: Be Organized

I cannot stress to you how important organization is to time management. Your brain needs to be organized, your life needs to be organized, and you need to be organized enough to develop systems to stay organized. I also find that an organized desk and home help my brain to be less cluttered.

Sometimes when I find myself overwhelmed, I take time to organize my workspace or my kitchen because I can't think amongst clutter and scribbled notes. Organizing your space, however, will also help you to know where everything is or goes, which makes doing anything more efficient than looking for something for thirty minutes.

What helps me dress for the day and get out on time is having my closets organized by sleeve length and then by color. When I'm getting ready in the morning after I check the weather, I know where to shop based on my mood, my schedule for the day, and the temperature. Find the tools and organization systems that work best for you and put them to work to help you manage your time.

Step #7: Develop a Best Practices and Stick to It

Once you find a rhythm that keeps the momentum of your day running so that you can accomplish all you need to do, keep doing what you're doing. I like to keep notepads and pens all over the house because I know that I can rely on them to make sure I stay on task and on top of what I need to do and when. The notepad by the couch is there so that if I need to trim the cat's nails, I write it there. Then I am reminded when I'm sitting and the cat is sitting while being blissfully unaware of what's going to happen to her. It's a good thing she can't read. I also use that notepad to remind myself of things I need to do when I get up off the couch and before I go to bed. My sit-on-the-couch time is my most tired and brain-vulnerable time so assuming I'll remember something when I get up is stupid. I won't. I'm exhausted from making time my b*tch all day!

The notebook in my bathroom is there for things that I need to know first thing in the morning or for things I think of when I'm putting my makeup on. The notepad in the kitchen is one of the largest because I spend a lot of time in the kitchen. That one reminds me if I need to thaw meat out for dinner two days beforehand, if I need to start a crock pot or the oven at a weirdly early time of the day, if there are deviations to the norm at school (dress-up days or field trips) or errands I need to run, and whose turn it is to sit in the "middle" at dinner.

That last item is so dumb. My kids have it in their minds that the middle barstool at the kitchen island is the place of royalty or something. There are three stools on one side and one that is on a side that is perpendicular so, a total of four. While "the middle" is in the middle of the three barstools on that side, when it's just them and me, it's not in the middle anymore because I sit on the adjacent side. Like I said, dumb, but I have to make a chart, so we don't get confused about whose turn it is to sit in "the middle". Whatever. It's not an effective use of time or energy to fight so I make the chart.

There are notebooks in more obvious places, like on my desk in my home office and on my desk in my work office, but each serves a purpose. There are three lists lined up on my refrigerator as well. The one on the left is the weekly menu, the one in the middle is the grocery list, and the one on the right is the Sam's Club list. After completing these lists in tandem, I have made it a best practice to photograph them together with my cell phone in case a list gets lost in the cavern that is my handbag or in case someone asks me what's for dinner, and I've forgotten.

Lists are a simple but very effective time and task-management tool. Putting things down on lists frees up your brain of the clutter, and allows you to focus on the tasks at hand.

Step #8: Be Efficient

While many of these steps will help you to be more efficient, generally being efficient in all that you do will help you use time more wisely. If you realize that a process isn't working well, find a different way of doing it. I once had employees who were taking the oddest steps to upsize their paper calendars from legal to tabloid size for residents, and when I heard about it, I asked why they didn't do it the easy way. "I didn't know you could do that," they said. "I'm so glad you showed me, I wish I'd known sooner!" I walked away, shaking my head and wondering what all their former managers had been doing.

There have been so many instances where I have helped others work smarter and not harder, and it's such a great thing to be able to figure out those shortcuts and help others do it as well. If something isn't working or doesn't make sense, stop doing it, and find a better solution. My husband is the love of my life, but I can't say he's the role model for efficiency.

Recently, the snowblower broke, and my husband was in search of a part to fix it. "I think we should go to the place down the hill. That's where I had to go for the lawnmower part," he said. Stupidly assuming he knew what he was talking about, I went with him only to be told they didn't have it.

As my husband turned to leave, I asked the guy behind the counter, "Do you know of any other place in town that might have it?"

"You might want to check with (store)."

"Thanks!" I said as we walked out.

In the car, I said with more of a tone than was probably needed, "Were you going to ask him if there was somewhere else that had it?"

"No. I hadn't thought to ask," he responded flippantly. "That was a waste of time. Why wouldn't you call before coming down here? Let's call this other place before you drive thirty minutes over there only to find out they don't have it either," I huffed as I dialed the number.

In my mind, running all over town seemed an inefficient waste of time and gas. While I don't like to step on my husband's manhood by second-guessing him or telling him how to manage his life, I cannot stand inefficiency and wasting resources, so I tend to take over when the systems are failing. Take this lesson from our wandering and streamline your processes so you don't waste time… or fight or dumb crap with your spouse.

Step #9: Don't Waste Snippets of Time

You can accomplish so much more than you think in a free five to ten minutes. Granted, you wouldn't start a big work project ten minutes before you leave for the day, but you can always find ways to use small snippets of time in your day to check items off your to-do list.

In the morning before I leave at 7:10 am to take the kids to school and head to work, sometimes I will find myself with an extra five to ten minutes to spare before go time. I look around and think about what I can do in that timeframe. Many times, I tidy up the living room blankets, fold laundry, clean the kitchen counters, or start my menu for the next week. I love to come home to a tidy house. Do I consider sitting down? No. A body doing tasks stays doing tasks, and I keep checking tasks off my to-do list all day until I'm so tired I can't function... that usually happens right after dinner.

> *Dick and Jane had a little more chaos in their lives than they would like, and it was starting to get stressful. "Joy told me that she had a stretch of nine days off from school coming up," Jane mentioned in a slight panic to Dick. "Do you know about this?" Jane asked her husband. "I thought the*

school sent home a calendar at the beginning of the year. Where is it?" he asked.

"Ugh! I think I left it in my office at work with my planner," said Jane in a huff. "I have some big projects at work next week, and I can't be home. What does your next week look like?" she asked Dick.

"I have some VPs from headquarters in next week, so I need to be in the office too."

Annoyed with being caught off guard, Jane called Sandy to complain about the potential issue. "Don't the schools post their calendars on their websites? Can't you check his schedule there?" asked Sandy.

"Oh, probably. I didn't think about that," she replied.

"And Jane," Sandy started, "You know I adore you, but you have got to switch from a paper planner to a digital calendar; your life will be so much easier, and you won't have surprises like this anymore."

> "I'll have to think about it. Maybe you can show me at work on Monday… when I have to be in the office when my daughter is on spring break!" she said with a laugh.
>
> "Thanks, lady. I gotta go so I can call around to see if one of the grandparents can watch Joy."

Achieving an A+ in time management is not an easy feat. However, if you can follow the steps and make time your b*tch, you can do almost anything.

HE SAID

She: On a scale of 1-10, how effectively do you manage your time, 10 being completely organized with your time management?

He: I'd say a four, depending on what day of the week it is. During the work week, I'm a lot more productive than I am on my time off.

She: Where do you struggle with time management?

He: In my time off when I don't have something that needs to be done, like work, then I don't have good organization of my time. When I'm working and only have a set amount of time to use, I can be a lot more effective. If I have a huge amount of time to get things done, I piss it away pretty quickly.

She: Weird. How do you prioritize your to-do list?

He: Probably by what I'm told.

She: *(Laughing)* But when you're at your house with your to-do lists, how do you prioritize those?

He: The number one thing is always what I want to do. That's how I prioritize. Not usually by what needs to be done. If what I want to do is what I need to do, then, it usually goes pretty quickly.

She: And how often does that happen?

He: Not very often. Like last week when I changed my oil, I needed to do it, so I made it a priority and was able to do it very quickly.

She: But you like doing that.

He: No, not necessarily. I'd rather not have to do it, but I've done it enough times and have all the right equipment.

She: How many tasks can do you at once, and how many do you think could you max out doing at the same time?

He: Depends on what it is. At work, I can do a lot of things at once.

She: Like how many, and what are they?

He: Well at work I'm usually driving around, using the radio, listening for things that are happening, watching people that are around, reading and running plates on my computer...

She: You can run plates while you're driving?

He: Yep.

She: So, like three or four things?

He: More than that probably. It's infinite.

She: What!? I don't know if I believe that.

He: At that job. My brain is wired to do that job. But at home on my days off I used to multitask. I used to work out while watching TV, cleaning the house, and doing laundry.

She: So, what has changed then?

He: Because I don't have days off there anymore.

She: Oh. But you have days off at my house. Can't you multitask at my house?

He: I could, but I usually get sucked into the TV.

She: Oh-ho! Okay. Why have you chosen to use a paper calendar to organize your life instead of a digital one?

He: Because I'm a Boomer, and I don't like doing it on the computer. I'm not a technology guy, and a lot of the people I work with are the same way.

She: Are they old?

He: Yeah, they're all my age, and we like pulling out our calendars and looking at them. There's just something about having something tangible that makes you feel good.

She: But don't you see how inefficient that is?

He: Not everything is about efficiency. It takes a lot more to go into your phone and enter that stuff than it is to write it in my notebook.

She: Yeah, but you leave your notebook places sometimes.

He: That should tell you how important it is to me. Organization like that, planning, and that stuff isn't that important to me.

She: How organized are you, and what are you most organized at?

He: I'm not organized.

She: I know. What do you think is your best area of organization?

He: Um… um… probably my workouts, I suppose. How I organize them seems to work for my body.

She: But that's just a routine.

He: No, most people write their gains and workouts down, and I don't need to do that.

She: Because that's important to you.

He: Yeah.

She: Do you know where everything you need is located?

He: No. There's stuff that I cannot find that is important, but I haven't been able to find it for a long time.

She: *(Giggling)* Okay. You're proving my point.

He: I would still like to know where that stuff is because it's important.

She: When you forget to bring your meds or night guard to my house, why don't you utilize the pink luggage tag with the packing list that I put on your overnight bag?

He: I don't know. I'm lazy. It's hard because when you're always in the moment, you aren't thinking about the future which is bad, I guess.

She: But aren't you thinking toward the future when you're packing to come up here?

He: Not really. I usually do it at the last minute before I leave. I fold up some gym clothes and stuff them in the bag…

She: Because the gym clothes are important to you, but the other things that are actually very important to you are not packed?

He: Well, I remembered everything this time because I took my meds, and then I immediately took the bottle and stuck it in my bag. But sometimes I take my meds and set it down thinking I'm going to grab it, but then I forget.

She: But why can't you just add the one extra step to check the tag with the list on it? It would take two seconds.

He: It just doesn't work. I don't know why. All I can think of is that in the moment I'm distracted by a podcast or something on my phone…

She: But that's not important like not forgetting your medicine is important.

He: There's something in my brain that doesn't worry about not having something that I need. I've always been able to adapt and deal with anything that happens so there's not that fear or worry there that would train my brain to not have to deal with it. I think that you need motivation that identifies what should be important, but I just don't have that, and I don't know why.

She: Why don't you like to ask someone at a store where something is located if you're not 100% sure of where it is?

He: Because I don't want to have contact with people.

She: *(Laughing)* It's not like "I don't want to look stupid"?

He: It has nothing to do with that. I just don't want to talk to anybody.

She: Why?

He: I don't know why.

She: UGH! Okay. That's weird. Why would you rather go to a parts store to ask if they have a part instead of calling ahead first?

He: In that case, I do like to have contact with people.

She: But you didn't call that last time we went, and they didn't have it.

He: I just assumed they would. To me, I didn't think it was a big deal. I know it's not efficient, but it's something to do. It's better than sitting at home watching TV.

She: Yeah, but I had things to do, and I had to go with you.

He: I'm sorry I put you out. It was time for us to spend together; I didn't think it would be a big issue.

She: It's not a big issue. I'm trying to make a point.

He: You're talking to the wrong kind of person about it.

She: Yes, but I'm talking to the kind of person who needs help which could be where some people are coming from.

He: I can't see a scenario, other than the military, where people are yelling at me that it would motivate me to do something…

She: Okay, let me finish the questions. How does it make you feel when we are together, and I ask a store associate for help?

He: It doesn't make me feel anything.

She: It doesn't embarrass you?

He: No, not at all.

Two people could not be more different than my husband and me when it comes to time management and pretty much everything in life. Luckily for him, however, he has me to assist where he needs assistance. The important takeaway from his perspective is that you will not be able to make time your b*tch and be effective at time management, organization, and efficiency unless it is an important priority to you.

Time is the only resource that you can't ever get more of, so using it most efficiently will only make your life easier and more productive. Adjusting here and there can have a very significant impact on your daily life, stress level, and enjoyment of your relationships. Using the methods discussed earlier could have other side benefits like how delegating tasks to your children can teach them responsibility and how asking your spouse for help can decrease your level of frustration and resentment in your relationship.

Getting more done in the same amount of time will change your life, and if you usually have trouble sleeping… you won't anymore if you make time your b*tch and keep moving until you are just too tired to move off the couch, where you may or may not fall asleep and start drooling on yourself out of satisfied exhaustion.

Chapter 4:

Beware of the Green-Eyed FOMO Monster

SHE SAID

FOMO. Fear of Missing Out, or jealousy, in a simpler term. It happens to the best of us by seeping into our lives through social media and television ads or simply by opening our eyes and seeing what others possess. Hannibal summed it up amazingly in his creepy but memorable line: "How do we begin to covet, Clarice? We covet what we see," in the movie *Silence of the Lambs*. How can we not start to want what others have if it's always in our faces, day after day, hour after hour?

Always chasing something that has no end will only breed unsettled dissatisfaction. Yes, it's human nature to be jealous, but recognizing the issue and finding ways to overcome it grants a greater power than having all "the things" ever can. Why? Because happiness often hides in contentment, but contentment only comes to those who have the introspective fortitude to dig deep for it.

Career FOMO

When starting your professional life, it seems as though everyone is lined up on the same level playing field. Sure, some people have more prestigious degrees than others, but everyone has to start somewhere. As time passes, some people climb that corporate ladder so effortlessly, others struggle up the rungs, and some even fall off. When you're the one toward the middle or bottom of the ladder, and all you can do is look up and wish you were higher, you have a case of career FOMO. That's where I found myself for the past several years, trying to hop sideways and up like how they advise you to run in a zig-zag if you're being chased by an alligator or some other scary predator with bad zig-zag skills. Hopping in a zig-zag pattern up the corporate ladder is as awkward, difficult, and as frustrating as it sounds.

My professional life started just as it was supposed to. I went to college, got a BS degree, and got a job in a cubicle. About six months after I started that job, I left and started my own business. Twelve years later, I got divorced, which meant no more being my own boss. I needed benefits, and so I went back to an office job which was not as easy as I thought it should be. Because my skillset didn't align perfectly with the job descriptions of the positions I wanted, I had to start at a job that didn't pay well. Job beggars without benefits can't be choosy, right?

About five years and a handful of jumps up the corporate ladder later, I felt like I was close to where I thought I should be for my age and experience, so I started applying for C-suite positions. Social media was polluting my mind into thinking that since all my friends were getting C-Suite level jobs that paid six figures, I was somehow falling behind the curve and needed to catch up. Why did it seem so easy for everyone else to get the jobs that they wanted, and I couldn't? I interviewed hard for over a year and was so close to getting the job I wanted as a co-executive director. The day I got turned down for that job as one of the two finalists, I ugly cried so hard my magnetic eyelashes came off... eyelashes that had withstood a 66 mph rollercoaster but were no match for my literal downpour of disappointment. After trying my very best and hardest, I came to the decision that it was time to reassess my goals and what I wanted for my life... and to look at a better adhesive for my eyelashes.

While I enjoyed my job at the nonprofit, there were no more advancement opportunities, and the pay left much to be desired. I was frustrated, stressed, and exhausted from the highs and lows of the interviewing roller coaster. One morning, my mother called me to tell me that my uncle had passed away. His sudden passing reminded me that life isn't always about money; it's about the people in your life and making sure you have time for them. In that moment of pause that inadvertently happens when you lose a loved one, I realized that the job I held allowed me adequate pay to survive but also the freedom and flexibility to take care of my family in the way that I felt necessary to ensure happiness at home.

Do you ever think that sometimes, when you try so hard to get something and you don't get it, maybe you weren't supposed to have it? Maybe I wasn't supposed to get a different job. Once I decided to stay at my job and make the most of it while cutting back on expenditures to be able to afford life on the salary I was making, it changed my whole outlook and my mood. The situation hadn't changed, but my perspective had, and I found myself finally able to lasso and control the career FOMO monster.

Regaining control over my situation by regulating how I was reacting to and handling it gave me a sense of peace. The people who were important to me were able to receive the attention they deserved, and I realized that job satisfaction is more than just about a paycheck and a title.

If we spend a third of our lives at work, we need to assess what our priorities are regarding our goals for our careers. These goals can either drive you insane, make you stressed and crabby, or they can make you feel good about the work that you do, the people you have time for, and the decisions you've made to be content, happy, and fulfilled.

Take some time to dig deep into how your career aspirations make you feel, what you're getting and not getting, and how your life outside of your career is impacted by your aspirations. A deep, submersive dive may lead you to find some clarity and happiness too.

Houses, Cars, and Stuff FOMO

Can you ever have enough stuff? I suppose the people who run the show Hoarders know that you can, but how do you know when you've "arrived"? What and whom are you chasing? Sometimes we can find ourselves chasing things without ever stopping to understand why we are doing it or what the endpoint looks like.

In many instances, the things we aspire to have are really just brand names that we hear about and associate with success and wealth. Did you ever play that kids' paper fortune teller game (aka "cootie catcher") with the tabs you pull up to reveal the answers when the game stops? I remember putting cars on those tabs like Ferrari, Lamborghini, and Porsche. I'd never even seen one of these cars, but from a young age, I thought they were the pinnacle of something. But why? Who puts these ideas into our heads, sets the bar so unattainably high, and attaches happiness to that unachievable goal?

How many wealthy people do you know who are truly happy? Personally, I know zero. I even heard one couple say how left out they felt because they were the only co-owners of a sports team who did NOT have a private jet. Private jet FOMO… hmmm… that's beyond my comprehension, but it proves that even though you may still be at an aspirational level to most, you can still suffer from stuff FOMO and be unhappy.

Unlike the Pharaohs of Egypt, we know that you can't take your stuff with you when you die so why the constant drive for material things? Stuff, so much stuff. Our throwaway society has programmed us to "need" more things because it's almost cheaper to buy new than to fix things. The cheaper the crap has become, the less we value what we buy. Furthermore, the lower costs allow us to buy more crap, which, ironically, makes it literal crap.

> *Dick and Jane had gone out a few times for dinner with Dick's work friend Bob and his wife Mary, and they were excited to have been invited over to the new house they just built. As Dick and Jane pulled up to their new friends' large home with an attached four-car garage, Dick jokingly said, "Geez, I'm not sure if we're cool enough to hang out with them."*
>
> *"Stop it, Dick. They're our friends. I'm sure they don't care what we drive or how much we make." Jane replied as they got out of their minivan.*
>
> *"Oh hey, guys!" shouted Bob from the porch.*

"Don't park that ugly minivan on my driveway," Bob said in jest as he walked over to shake Dick's hand.

After a nice dinner of chit-chat and good food, Dick and Jane got in their vehicle to drive home. "I feel like maybe Bob and Mary should give us a bag of canned goods when we leave. Their house makes me uncomfortable like we're not good enough to be there and that we need handouts like donated food," Dick grumbled as he drove a little more aggressively than usual.

"Yeah, I mean, I sort of thought that they were on the same socioeconomic playing field as we were, but clearly, they make way more than we do. Their community even has an indoor pool." Jane agreed.

When they got back and walked inside their home, all they saw was what it wasn't. The house needed updates, the carpet needed replacing, and their garage wasn't even attached to their house. The house they had once loved and celebrated had turned into a symbol of not-good-enough-anymore. "I'm tired. I'm going to bed," Dick grumbled to Jane as he walked upstairs. With a big sigh, she followed silently behind him.

The next day after school, Joy's friend Poppy came over to study. "Do you want to stay for supper, Poppy?" Jane asked.

"Oh yeah! I love it here. Joy, you're so lucky to have a mom who cooks and a house that's always clean. My house is always a mess, and I never get homemade food, like ever!" declared Poppy as she got up to steal a warm roll that Jane had just pulled from the oven.

That evening when Dick and Jane turned off their bedside lamps, Jane turned to Dick with, "You know, I think we have it pretty good. We raised our family in his house, and while it's not as big as Bob and Mary's house, it's filled with love, and I'm okay with that."

"You've got a good point, love." Dick agreed.

"Plus, this house has you in it, and Joy and that's all I need to be happy," he continued as he cuddled his wife.

"Ooh! And I'd sure hate to have to clean that house!" Jane joked as she gave in to her husband's love-laden overtures.

When we moved up to the Duluth, MN area, we bought the house I said I was going to die in. I absolutely loved everything about that house. It was enormous with its gorgeous wrap-around porch, five garage stalls, a theater in the basement, a paved parking lot, and five wooded acres. I had arrived! It was everything I'd ever wanted in a house, but oddly enough, I found myself more miserable than ever when I had it.

Now that's just not right. What was wrong with me? I had everything I thought I was trying to get when it came to a house and cars and all the tangible things that I thought I wanted. Turns out, stuff can't make you happy. Who knew? After one year in my dream house, I moved out during my divorce into the smallest house I have ever lived in. Most people find themselves moving forward and upward not backward and downward in their lives, and I was struggling in my move backward.

As I enjoyed the glider rocker on my dream porch for the last time, I remember telling myself, "The rustling of the leaves in the wind that I love will sound exactly the same from this porch as they do from the tiny three-season porch at my new home." I was giving up all the things I thought I wanted for the chance to find happiness and satisfaction on a deeper level.

While I still have to drive by that house almost every day on my way to the kids' school, I try to remind myself why I gave up the things that I gave up and why. When my children bring up that house when we pass, I tell them that it's not the size of the house but the people in it that are important. It's good for me to remind them of that fact because sometimes I need to hear that reminder too.

Many of the people that I work with, my amazing coworkers who are in the same we-don't-get-paid-enough position at my nonprofit, are some of the most content, genuine, and happy people. Some of them make so little that they qualify for the social services help that we offer other people, so why are they so happy? From the outside, they seem to be struggling and don't have all the things that many people work so hard for and value. Many of them have been through very difficult life-changing situations and have been given the gift of perspective. This gift allows them to find joy in their work because they love helping others through the challenges that they too have faced, and it's inspiring to witness. I suppose if they can be happy, so can I.

HE SAID

She: Would you rather have a job you hated and made a ton of money, or would you rather have a job you loved but did not pay well?

He: One that I loved.

She: Why?

He: Why do anything just for money?

She: So, you don't have to struggle.

He: Granted, if it didn't pay the bills, that would be a different story. I'd rather have something I liked doing and felt good about than do something I didn't feel good about that paid more money. Life isn't about money.

She: What was the job that you've had that you loved the most?

He: Being a stripper.

She: Why?

He: Because it was fun, there were a lot of benefits... like access to women... for where I was at in life, it was exciting and different, and it made me feel like a small-town celebrity. It was just fun *(grinning with nostalgia)*.

She: Did you get paid well for that job?

He: Yeah.

She: If you had to rate your job satisfaction with your current job 1-10, what would it be and why?

He: Nine because it gives me purpose and pays me well, and it's going to be over soon.

She: Do you wish you got paid more, or are you happy with the salary you receive for the work that you do?

He: I'm happy with it.

She: Have you ever had house FOMO?

He: No.

She: Why?

He: Because material things don't matter to me, and I don't compare myself to other people on how good my house is.

She: What about career or title FOMO?

He: Nope. I love what I do.

She: Car or vacation FOMO?

He: Um, no.

She: You never wanted to take more vacations like other people?

He: I take a fair amount of vacations.

She: Well, you do now. How about before like when you had to work overtime?

He: No, I had a lot of other things I liked to do. I never felt like I was missing out on anything.

She: Hmm. What do you think that people should prioritize when it comes to a job or career: happiness or money?

He: Happiness as long as the bills are paid. Find something that pays the bills and that you feel good about doing. Something where you don't come home upset and bring that unhappiness into your personal life. You don't want to do that.

She: How can people avoid FOMO with stuff or careers?

He: Be appreciative of what you have, and don't focus on other people. Don't spend your time looking at other people unless it motivates you. The moment you feel unhappy because of FOMO, you need to ignore that or be happy for the other person for what they have but don't hold yourself to a standard that isn't your standard.

I remember having a conversation with my ex-husband where I asked him if he would rather have a job that paid well but that he hated, or a job that paid terribly but he loved. His response surprised me when he said, "I can't answer that because I've never had a job that I loved." I don't think that most people could say that they love their jobs, and here I was with a job that I loved but it just did not pay well.

The FOMO mindset, as a result of seeing others on social media having it better than you, has turned our society into the worst case of Keeping Up with the Joneses ever. Before people's worlds became so big, many seemed happier with the things that they had because they weren't constantly being reminded of all the things that they didn't. Maybe much of the reason that my hubby doesn't suffer from FOMO is due to his complete lack of social media… or I suppose it could be all the concussions he's had too.

If you find that you are running toward a goal that you don't see the end to, maybe it's time to stop and visualize what you are or should be running toward. People who work more and see their families less face a higher risk of having regrets. Many times, the higher paying the job, the more stress it induces which can be a detriment to physical health and the health of personal relationships.

While I don't give my husband a ton of credit in some of the skillsets I'm teaching in this book, I do envy how easily he comes by his certainty of what is important. FOMO is a fight I take on almost daily, but I hope to suck less and less at it with you as I strive to refocus from the external to the int

Chapter 5:

Bullies, They Aren't Just for Kids

SHE SAID

Unfortunately, with age doesn't always come maturity. If you were ever bullied as a child, you know how terrible that feels, but it can feel just as terrible if you get bullied as an adult. Adult bullying can take many forms, it can be social media harassment, mean girls at work, a group of peers talking about you behind your back, or even racial or cultural insensitivity.

Workplace Bullies

When there are no higher authority figures like school administration or teachers to help you with your bullying problems, how are you to handle them in a mature, adult fashion?

One of my friends seems to keep running into the mean girl situation at every job, and she doesn't understand why, but I too have encountered this issue. I had a very short-term job that ended abruptly because my female boss had some self-esteem issues. "I knew this was going to happen," my husband said at the time of the incident.

"Why?!" I said through tears of shock.

"Your boss was not going to put up with how much attention you were getting in that male-dominated industry. She's jealous, and it was always going to end this way." While his reasoning may have been the truth of the situation, it didn't make any logical sense to be fired over.

Jealousy seems to be the largest cause of workplace bullying. People can be jealous of you for any number of reasons, probably for many of the FOMO reasons mentioned in the last chapter but it can also be jealousy about relationship status, looks, how much you get paid, or how many more freckles you have than they do. The list is endless because the reasons don't have to make sense to anyone but the bully. People can be mad at you for the stupidest reasons that you have no control over, but that's life, and we need to find constructive ways to manage it.

Many people who are mean to others are that way because they have a lack of happiness and satisfaction in their own lives. People who are happy and content aren't mean to other people for no reason. Why would they? Like you, I don't enjoy being bullied or being talked down to as an adult, but when it does happen, I try to remind myself that the bully probably has something going on in their personal life that is making them miserable. Since the only part of these interactions that I can control is my reaction to the issue, I try not to let their issues affect how happy and content I am in my situation and life.

Right, but how do you work with someone who has an irrational disdain for your very existence? If your tormentor is at the same level as you at work, try to meet with that person privately and ask them one-on-one some of the following questions:

1. I've noticed that you've been a little on edge lately. Is everything okay?
2. I like my job and want to do my best, and I'm open to suggestions on how to improve. Is there anything that you think I could improve on?

Approaching in this way shows the other party that you are aware of an issue and will call out bad behavior without being unprofessional. It also allows the other party to speak their mind with open-ended questions that don't necessarily make accusations or threats.

If the right-to-the-source method doesn't make the situation better, then it's time to go to the next level above them – their supervisor. Scheduling a meeting with the supervisor gives you time to calm down and organize your thoughts instead of just bursting into his office like a psycho, which I have done. If you handle the situation with tact and professionalism, the issue is more likely to seem legitimate and something that will make it easier for the supervisor to solve.

If the situation still does not improve, then all you can do is smile through the annoyance and treat that person with respect. If they see that they aren't getting a reaction out of you, they'll likely stop, just like juvenile bullies do. You never know, if you can remain emotionally neutral with the offender, they may eventually come to you for friendship because they've alienated everyone else. It does happen, but it's rare.

Social Media Trolls

Social media has made it so easy for unhappy trolls to prey on anyone, anywhere, and at any time. Oftentimes social media trolls don't have all the information and just make snap comments and judgments without knowing the facts because they have nothing better to do.

> *When Joy was little, Jane decided to join the PTA at Joy's school. One year during board elections, Jane found herself being nominated for President because of her bubbly personality and natural*

leadership abilities. She led the organization for a few years when disaster struck. It had come to her attention that the treasurer of the PTA, someone she called a friend, had been stealing money from the organization for years.

After Jane filed a report with the local police, the news got wind of the scandal, and the rest of the PTA board was being hounded for inside stories. "Ladies, I will handle the media since I filed the report and am already tied to the investigation. Don't say anything, and I'll bear the brunt of it," she explained.

As a leader in the organization, Jane was prepared to do what great leaders do: they stand with integrity and professionalism and don't run away. When the story ran, the social media trolls came after her with their pitchforks raised and called out where she worked, saying that she was supposedly a smart person and should have known better... people were calling for her head.

"Dick, I don't understand why people are being so mean. I'm not the one who did anything wrong!"

she sobbed into her husband's shirt. "I wish you'd quit that organization. It's so much work and look where all of your volunteering has gotten you. I hate to see you so upset," he said with anger in his voice for all of the people hurting his love.

"I can't quit now. It would look like I'm running away. No, I said I would stay and make sure that the PTA got back on its feet again, and that's what I plan to do." Jane said with conviction. Through conversations with the media, the principal, and the superintendent, Jane did her best to keep her cool and do the best she could as the leader of the organization.

Eventually, the treasurer was arrested, jailed, and then taken to court and found guilty. The focus shifted off Jane and onto the real criminal where the focus should always have been. Jane stayed on and helped facilitate a new fundraiser that left the organization financially stable again. Coming through a traumatic time of cyberbullying made Jane a stronger person and a better leader.

After my first book came out, one of the local television stations came to my house and spent two hours interviewing me for two stories: one about my book, and the other about my volunteer work in the community. When the volunteering story ran on the news, and the TV station put it on their Facebook page, an internet troll jumped on the post and wrote this message:

> "I don't understand... I've seen this person on the news several times lately. I've seen so many amazing women do all she has and more and don't get all the ego petting this woman has. I've met her in passing a few years ago I didn't see compassion I saw her parading around the place with arrogant demeanor though. This is a trait I don't think is impressive or deserves rewarding. There are many humble and special people in this world that never get a thank you."

I was insulted and furious when I read her message to which I did not respond. Who did she think she was? I don't know who she is and where she thinks she met me, but I do know that my work bestie told me that when she first saw me, she jumped to certain conclusions about me based on how I dress and that I'm confident. After getting to know me, she has come to realize how wrong she was.

There was this time when she was having a technology issue in her office, and I explained to her how she could fix it. After a brief stare of shock, she said, "I can't believe you walk around in heels and look like that and are smart too!" She can get away with saying things like that because our friendship is weird, but if even my good friend started out making assumptions about me simply based on the resting b*tch face some people say I have, then why wouldn't I assume that others who don't know me wouldn't do that also?

If you are faced with a social media bully, you can report them, unfriend or block them, or ask a page admin to remove their comment. It's a good rule of thumb not to engage someone in a virtual battle because it never goes anywhere but south. Or you could just avoid all social media like my husband does.

While the social media comment bothered me, I could see how someone who had some personal issues combined with some biased assumptions might respond in that manner. I don't condone that kind of social media bullying, but trying to understand the why of bullying will oftentimes give you the grace you need to look past it and move on.

Racial Bullying and Cultural Insensitivity

Being born in South Korea but being reared in rural Wisconsin was the perfect storm for racial bullying. I have certainly had my fair share of racial bullying and cultural insensitivity over the years, but it first started in my junior year of high school when a small group of senior boys decided to make it their mission to follow me around every day and yell racial slurs at me. To this day, I can't repeat them; they're too painful.

While racial intolerance was never again as bad as that one year in high school, it has never stopped happening. When I was with my first husband at his parents' lake home in northern

Wisconsin, we went to the public boat launch to put their pontoon in for the season. On the dock parallel to the boat launch sat a young white boy and his father. I was in the boat, and as I floated by the pair, the boy said to his dad, "Look Dad! A Chinese girl!"

For sh*t's sake. I mean, I know we were in the middle of nowhere Wisconsin in a town of 330, but teach your kids some cultural sensitivity. When we moved to Duluth from the Twin Cities, we had an air conditioner repair man over to assess our mini split unit. On the mantle beneath the air conditioner was a carved wooden dragon that my first husband and I had purchased on a vacation to Duluth one fall at an import store. I think it was from Indonesia. Regardless, I was working in my home office and could hear their conversation in the great room. "That's a cool dragon. Did your wife bring it with her when she came over?" Had I just heard that? He thought I was fresh off the boat from Asia! I yelled from my office, "I'm adopted!" He was never asked to come back to do work at our house.

Some of these interactions are almost humorous if they weren't so offensive. I share these cultural insensitivities with you to highlight them as a form of adult bullying. Well, bullying adjacent. Ignorance when it comes to someone's race can be just as insulting as calling them names intentionally.

When it comes to racial intolerance, I urge people to become more culturally aware, or please think before speaking to someone regarding race, gender, or anything that you are not 100% sure of. If you are the one being bullied, try to remain calm and respond with something informative and dignified… or something witty if you're great on the spot, which I usually am not in these situations.

In any bullying situation, the most important thing to remember is that you control the response, and the response can shut down the bullying or add fuel to the raging fire. Rising above and being the better person who offers steadfastness and calm to a bully shows a level of maturity that is very counterintuitive but aspirational. Try to keep in mind that behind every bully is some sort of trauma, unhappiness, or self-loathing, so let that fact help guide you to a place of grace.

HE SAID

She: Have you ever bullied someone as an adult?

He: Yeah, probably.

She: What was the situation?

He: I get very irritated when people aren't carrying their own weight or aren't working as hard as you are in a team setting.

She: How does that translate into bullying though?

He: When that happens, you start to treat them differently and make situations uncomfortable for them to get them to quit because you don't want to deal with their nonsense. I did that in the Army too.

She: You wanted people to quit?

He: Yeah, sometimes with people like that, you have to take an extra load on. I don't mind doing that, but it can get irritating.

She: Huh. Okay. Have you ever been bullied as an adult and what was the situation?

He: I don't think so.

She: No, never?

He: I don't think so.

She: How about as a child?

He: Oh yeah.

She: *(Deadpan)* Can you explain that?

He: I used to have a speech impediment that I used to get made fun of for until I couldn't take it anymore. I made myself stop doing it. I used to be afraid of being picked on as a child, but I forced myself to stop being afraid of stuff. I hate being afraid of things.

She: How did you get back at them?

He: I just started focusing my life on not being afraid of things, and then started doing things just to prove I wasn't afraid of them.

She: Okay, what was the thing you said the other day to the kids? "You need a friend to beat you up," or something… what was it?

He: You need an older person to beat up on you to toughen you up.

She: Like your friend from childhood. Did he bully you?

He: Maybe a little. I knew that he really liked me, but he wanted me to be at his level. People like that want you to be tough enough to hang out with them. I wanted to hang out with him, so I wanted to be tough enough.

She: What would he do? Push you down?

He: *(Laughing)* He'd do all kinds of stuff. He'd put the figure four headlock on me and roll down the terrace or kick and hit me…

She: In the face?!

He: *(Amused)* Oh yeah! Yeah, yeah.

She: *(Horrified)* And your family allowed this to happen?

He: My mom told me, "If you want to hang out with those kids, then I don't want to see you crying about it." So, I went off somewhere and cried about it until it didn't hurt as bad anymore. Eventually, you get to a point where it doesn't hurt.

She: So, did he stop doing it then?

He: No. He kept it up.

She: He kept doing it, regardless?

He: He did it until I fought back enough until it was more of an effort for him to get me. That was a life-changing event.

She: I wonder how much he's affected the person you are today.

He: A lot. Most people don't ever know what they can endure until they go past the point of just having to endure it. When you see people who are far and above superior, like athletes, they've been to that spot, and they know they can make it through. The more times you do that, the easier it is, and you don't fear it. You don't look for excuses to quit because you know you can do it and have been through worse.

She: So, sometimes bullying can be a good thing, is that what you're saying?

He: Oh, I totally think it is. It also helps you feel empowered when you can survive something like that – do things on your own and protect yourself – you don't have that victim mentality. That's the worst thing, the victim mentality that leads you to make excuses not to endure uncomfortableness.

I've always said, "You don't ever get better by being comfortable. You only get better by being uncomfortable. The more you are uncomfortable, the better you're going to be because you will be looking for ways to overcome that."

She: So, how would you explain how when I got racially bullied by older boys in school... how would I have overcome that in that situation?

He: What do you mean?

She: How would I have gotten to the point like you did with your friend and getting beat up? There was nothing I could do.

He: No, but you focus on making yourself stand out for positive reasons... like how you are super attractive. You show them that "despite how you treated me, I'm where I'm at now" and no one can touch you now. Now they're not even on your level anymore to where they could affect you.

She: So, use bullying to push yourself to be better, is that what you're saying?

He: I just think that you grow from it, but some people don't. Some people carry it with them their whole lives and are always unhappy because they can't get over it. When you can turn bullying into motivation, people can see that power in you.

She: Do you think that men or women are more likely to have and make workplace enemies, and why?

He: I think women are.

She: You don't have any enemies at work?

He: I've had some in the past, but I try not to make any enemies because I know what that can lead to. I think it happens when people feel like they're competing with someone else.

She: So, it's a woman thing.

He: Definitely. Women are way more competitive and way more vindictive, but guys can do it too if they don't like you. I've had women that hated me...

She: At work!?

He: Yeah, but I've always tried not to talk bad about them or give them any reason to come after me, but some people can't let that go, and they get burned. I don't like having enemies. Even if I don't agree with someone, I give them respect and the ability to not feel bad about themselves based on anything that I've done.

She: Why do you think women are more likely to have workplace enemies?

He: A lot comes from insecurity and where they find their value. Traditionally, women value attractiveness, and women hate other, more attractive women. Women see more attractive women, and they think there's no way that person could do anything without her looks like "I'd be where she is if I looked like that too." They can't accept the fact that the more attractive person might have some other abilities besides her looks: smarts, work ethic, or being nice. Lesser females always think more attractive women have gotten to where they are because of how they look, and the lesser females can't see past their jealousy. They'd rather see other women burn than give them any sort of acknowledgment for skills beyond looks.

She: What do you think someone should do if someone is bullying you at work?

He: You can't give them anything to give them ammunition against you. Bullies often push you to break, snap, or quit, and if you let them affect you, they can smell blood.

She: So, don't show weakness to them.

He: There have been times at work with certain people that I could sense were trying to do something to me, like this one guy who is always screwing with people. I knew that he got my friend worked up a few times. One time, I was going to the bathroom, and he was naked. He put his foot up by the urinal and asked, "What do you think of my balls?" I said, "I've seen better." After that, he never screwed with me again because he realized right away that I wasn't thrown off or intimidated by him, and it didn't faze me.

She: That's a weird thing to do.

He: He had no ammo to screw with me, but if I'd reacted like, "Hey! Get that thing away from me!" or something like that, he would constantly push my buttons. If someone is trying to push your buttons, just don't let them. Show them that they can't break you.

She: Why do you think people bully others on social media?

He: Because it's easy, there are no repercussions, and they can hide. It's the same thing. Most people would never dream of walking into a restaurant and going face-to-face with someone and smarting off to them because there's the possibility of immediate consequences. But if you're online, and no one can see you, you can say whatever you want, be as barbaric as you want, and there are no repercussions. That's not reality.

When I was a kid growing up, in my hometown, if you said something to someone and weren't going to back it up, you were going to get your ass handed to you. And everyone knew that; it was the code. Everyone knew the people that were at the top, and if you wanted to make a name for yourself, then you would have to go after the people that were at the top.

But now, in real life, you can't go out in public and smart off to people. You can get killed because people carry guns.

She: I thought you liked to get into fights.

He: Yeah, but you can't do that if you're not prepared to fight. When it comes to social media trolls, if you're going to swim in a pond with alligators, you can't get mad when one of them bites you.

She: So, do you think that it would be good for kids to be bullied so they can learn how to deal with it?

He: Yeah, within reason.

She: When you bring up bullying, everyone says, "I was bullied for xyz…" Everybody does.

He: Cause kids are cruel. If there are kids that don't understand interpersonal relationships, they have to learn them. If some kids don't have the proper adult role models, family, or religion, then they will learn interpersonal skills from how they interact with other kids.

If any time you were confronted with something, but nothing bad ever happened because it was stopped before any confrontation, then how do you deal with that in life because life is full of confrontation?

There's always going to be someone who doesn't agree with you, and how do you deal with that? If you haven't had that experience before, and someone comes up to you and says, "No, you're not doing that," and you really want to do it, you'll do something irrational, and it will end badly. As an adult, it will have higher ramifications than when you are younger.

For as much as we think adulting brings maturity, the reasons that adult bullying happens are very similar to the reasons that children bully each other: immaturity, ignorance, and jealousy. Bullying is something that will never go away no matter where you are or how old you get. I know because I saw it when I worked in senior living… with the seniors!

I remember a story that my husband told me about de-escalation at work as a police officer. There was a juvenile who was yelling and freaking out at the cops, and the tension was contagious. Other less seasoned officers were having a hard time staying cool, but my husband calmly walked up to the kid and asked if he needed a hug. That unexpected gesture caught him off guard, changed the mood, and the situation was resolved quickly and peacefully.

The only thing that you can control in negative situations is your reactions, or lack thereof. If you want to be a peacekeeper like my hubby, you'll need to learn to control your emotions. When you can do that, you can change the emotions of others around you. If you can meet a bully with a kind or empathetic response, you have the opportunity to change someone else's outlook for the better and give them one less reason to act out their unhappiness.

Chapter 6:

Stress is Stressful

SHE SAID

As someone who has been diagnosed with anxiety, I don't think that people should be given that diagnosis. Why? Because I think that people with anxiety are the majority and people without anxiety are the minority. The people who don't have it are the people who should be diagnosed as not having anxiety. What does anxiety have to do with stress and stress management? I'm a very high-stress person, but some of it is my fault... wait no, scratch that, all of it is my fault.

I put a lot of pressure on myself for pretty much everything, and even my hobbies are stressful. However, even if you are not as crazy as I am when it comes to expectations of oneself or all-encompassing hobbies that are work-like, everyone has stress they have to deal with as an adult. Life is never NOT stressful, and it never gets easier, it just changes.

When we were getting ready to move to Duluth, I got so stressed out that I got strep, shingles, and panic attacks all at the same time. I was a hot disaster. "Just breathe" or "Just calm down" are not helpful tidbits of advice; it's not that easy. When the move was over, I thought the stress symptoms would disappear, but the panic attack lasted three months. While being nauseous for that long was a great way to lose weight, eventually, I ended up going to the doctor who suggested therapy.

"I'm not a crazy mental person!" I said while having a crazy mental person-like meltdown at my first husband. "I'm a smart person, I should be able to control my body." While I wanted to be able to will away the constant sickness feeling, I eventually went to a therapist. After two sessions I was cured, and the subsequent sessions were more my asking her about her marriage and trying to solve her issues. I enjoyed that greatly because I love to meddle!

One of my children asked me recently if I was stressed. Racking my brain to think of what I might have been doing to elicit this question, I asked why. He happily presented me with a stress ball that he had found in his room because he thought I needed to have it. I don't think there exists any amount of stress balls that could be effective in reducing the amount of stress I have in my life. Ironically, the clutter of the stress balls would likely stress me out even further.

Given that we all have, or will have, a fair amount of stress in our adult lives, how can we find healthy and productive ways to deal with and manage it?

> *Dick was enjoying the promotion he had gotten at work, but the deadlines being imposed on him were starting to stress him out and make him almost unbearable to be around at home. Instead of spending time with Joy and Jane after dinner, Dick started to isolate himself in his home office with a glass of bourbon.*

While Jane wasn't a fan of the trend of less Dick and more alcohol, she was almost afraid to approach him because he had been short with her and Joy so much lately. She found herself trying to distance herself and Joy by taking Joy for walks after dinner or out for ice cream to avoid crabby Dick.

One evening after Jane and Joy had gone to bed, Dick found himself at the bottom of an empty bottle, and he told himself that he needed more to drown out the stress of his job. Getting into his car, he headed toward the liquor store. Five minutes later, his new car was smashed into a tree in a ditch not too far from the house.

Around midnight that evening, Jane was woken up by the sound of the phone. "Wait, what?!" she groggily replied as she realized Dick was not in the bed beside her. "I'll be right there!" Jane called her friend Sandy to come stay with Joy, and she made her way to the hospital to check on Dick.

"Dick! What were you thinking driving after you had that much to drink?" she yelled as she started to feel the tears sting her eyes.

"I don't know. I'm sorry. I think I may have a problem, Jane," Dick admitted.

"Well, I'm just glad you didn't get hurt worse," she sighed knowing he was okay. "I think I need to find a better way to manage the stress I'm having at work," Dick offered.

"I think that's for the best," Jane responded.

"We miss the old Dick," she muttered quietly.

When Jane took Dick home from the hospital, they came up with a plan for him to stop drinking and got him a gym membership where he would go when he felt stressed out. After a few months of heading to the gym after work and then coming home for dinner, he was a healthier, more energetic, stronger Dick. "Dick, I'm so proud of you, AND, I'm loving this new gym body of yours," she said with a wink before she gave his backside a playful slap.

Unfortunately, sometimes people turn to unhealthy ways of dealing with stress. Drugs and or alcohol may seem like a quicker fix, but they aren't healthy ways of managing stress. Furthermore, they will age you faster, which will add additional stress to the stress they were supposed to negate… so don't use those crutches. I have found that daily exercise is a great stress reducer, and so is stress baking. Before I started writing as a hobby, I would use my anxious energy to bake in double or triple batches. My garage freezer was always full of tasty treats that I was happy to give away to make other people smile.

If I find myself extremely angry and fired up about something, I put on my boxing gloves and punch the heavy bag my husband hung in the basement for me. The great thing about being able to punch an inanimate object is that you can put anyone's photo on that bag before you pulverize it.

Angry running is another way that I get myself to calm down if someone or something has pushed me over the edge, and there's nothing I can do about it. You don't know how fast you can run until you've angry run. Try it… it's kind of great. Think of angry running like when a toddler who is freaking out and throwing an epic tantrum. If you let them freak out until they wear themselves out, they eventually calm down, and so will you.

Another great way to deal with stress is to immerse yourself in a hobby. Hobbies are a way for you to refocus your brain toward something you enjoy. Also like with toddlers who are unhappy, if you can distract them with something they like, their mood will change very quickly. Reading, journaling, walking, sewing, baking, martial arts, dancing, playing an instrument… the possibilities are endless.

The wonderful thing about finding a healthy outlet to help manage stress is the side benefits. Many of these options will make you healthier, more interesting, or will produce something that can be eaten or given away.

HE SAID

She: Have you ever tried dealing with stress in unhealthy ways?

He: Oh, God yes.

She: If so, what were they?

He: Self-medicating in all sorts of ways like drinking and risky behavior...

She: What does that mean "medicating with risky behavior" when it comes to stress? Can you give me a "for instance"?

He: Like when my dad died, I went out and partied. That's when I was going to raves and doing out-of-control stuff. When my buddy Trent died, I went and rescued a dog that I couldn't even have. There are all kinds of things I've done. I've left one bad relationship and went right on to a new one.

She: How and or why did you stop using those behaviors as stress management tools?

He: Eventually you outgrow that stuff.

She: Do people? I don't think everyone outgrows drinking to deal with stress. Let's use drinking. When did you stop that?

He: The times that I've used drinking to deal with stress were not good because it didn't work.

She: What didn't work?

He: Drinking.

She: Well, duh! That's the whole point… that it's an unhealthy way to…

He: Well, it didn't work for me.

She: What things have caused you the most stress in your life?

He: Relationship stuff. They've been the hardest.

She: … or people dying?

He: No…

She: You just said that!

He: Failed relationships have been way more stressful to me than people dying.

She: Why?

He: Because I always internalized it, and it always felt like when people broke up with me, I thought it was all my fault and didn't look at the things that happened that weren't my fault. I'm an extreme person. When I'm upset about something, it seems like way bigger deal than it should be.

She: Yeah, because you're so calm all the time.

He: Yeah. When something bad happens to me, it drags out a lot of other things that I've been bottling up, which is common for a lot of men.

She: So, how did you deal with the end of relationships and that stress?

He: Being negative, screwing things up at work...

She: How did you deal with the last breakup?

He: In unhealthy ways.

She: But weren't you older? You said people grow out of unhealthy ways of dealing with stress.

He: I had to let it get really bad so I could see it from a different angle… It was a life-changing experience as far as understanding things in a bigger light and seeing the big picture and what life is about.

She: Would you say that while stressful and horrible at the time, it was a good thing to have gone through?

He: Oh yeah, definitely.

She: What did you learn from it?

He: You can't look at life with a naive lens. At a certain point, you realize that people do things for all kinds of different reasons, and people will manipulate situations to suit themselves best. The best thing you can do is be true to yourself and focus on the things that make you who you are and be proud of those things.

She: So, you came out of it realizing it wasn't all your fault?

He: Yeah, I came out realizing I'm okay with the person I am, and understanding who I am, and that's what I wanted. If you want to be the person you are, then be okay with that, and don't let other people make you feel like it's a bad thing.

She: Okay, how do you deal with stress on the job?

He: Part of it is not internalizing stressful situations at work. Looking at situations through a compassionate lens and asking, "How I can make it better?" Not looking at it like, "Everything just sucks and is horrible." Changing that thinking to "Maybe I can do something here to make it better" is how I manage it.

She: So, it's all about your perspective.

He: Yes, and looking at it like, "I can bring good energy into a situation that is horrible, and I don't have to bring that energy back out with me. I can leave it where it's at."

She: So, you don't have any stress at work?

He: No, I wouldn't say that. I have a lot of stress at work, especially with my body-worn camera.

She: That's what I'm trying to reference. When you encounter that stress at work, how do you deal with it? I don't see you drinking, I don't see you doing crazy stuff. How are you dealing with it?

He: My first inclination if I get a reprimand at work, is "This sucks! I'm not going to do sh*t anymore. They're just screwing with me. It's ridiculous!" But then within an hour, I'm like, "That's not who I am. I can't be like that. I don't want to be like that, and I'm not going to let anything that happens affect or change me because nothing is that big of a deal." I didn't do anything horrible. I can rationalize myself down.

She: How do you deal with stress in your personal life now?

He: I have gotten to a point where I know that I'm the one that controls the amount of stress in my life. So, I can push things out of my life that I know are going to be stressful. I'm not going to be with people that I know are going to cause me stress or do things that I know are going to set me up in a bad place...

She: What about the situation where someone stole your money from the bank? That was stressful. What was your coping mechanism?

He: My adaptability and my mindset of it not being that important. It sucks, but I can endure it because I've endured much worse things in my life. It's just money.

She: What do you think are some healthy ways that people can manage stress?

He: You have to have outlets.

She: Like hobbies?

He: All kinds of things, but it's 100% perspective. Being able to look at life in a certain way and figuring out what the most important things in your life are. If you can endure any kind of adversity and maintain your character, then you're not going to be stressed out as much.

She: What if I got diagnosed with terminal cancer? Would that stress you out?

He: I'd be sad, worried, and upset. But at the same time, I would look at it like, "What can I do to maintain my frame to make sure that she feels more comfortable and isn't worried about how I'm doing? How can I make it so I'm not a worry for her on top of the issues that are going on?"

She: Now, I'm not trying to feed you the answers, but I was talking about exercise or something like that to deal with stress.

He: But it's all perspective. When bad things happen, and people are stressed out, they want the pain to end.

She: Sometimes it's not bad though. There are different kinds of stress. Like regular life stress, and then there are the spikes in stress.

He: A lot of that has to do with diet and sleep. Let's say that you're unhappy at work, you're financially stressed, you have a crappy home life, where do you get your break at? Where do you have time to heal?

She: How. Would. You. Deal. With. That. Stress?

He: You tell me how you deal with it.

She: *(Laughs)* It's your scenario!

He: You have to make a plan to eliminate those stressors. If you're unhappy at work and are financially strapped, maybe try to get a job you're happier at and that makes more money.

She: So, working to solve the problem is one way to deal with it, yes?

He: Yeah, or maybe reassess if you can live the life you want to or if you need to get rid of things or get a less fancy car.

She: You're saying not to swallow stress, make changes to lessen the stress. Okay. Have you ever gone to therapy? For what?

He: Yes.

She: For what?

He: Relationship stuff.

She: What are your thoughts about therapy to deal with stress?

He: I think it's healthy to talk about stuff, and it's healthy to have another perspective, but at the same time, if you have a bad therapist, you might go down the wrong path.

She: So, you don't think that therapy is a good suggestion to help people manage stress?

He: It works for some people, but it doesn't work for everyone. A lot of times, it can lead people into victimhood and excuse-making. But sometimes it helps people become aware. It's one thing if you can take what you learn and retroactively make it fit into your life so you can be aware of these things when they happen so you can act accordingly, but it's another thing to use a diagnosis as a crutch not to move forward.

It depends on the therapist and how you use the information you learn. There are two kinds of people. Some people grow up with a sh*tty childhood but come out of it and make themselves better because they don't want to have to live like that anymore. But then you also have the people that perpetuate the issues because they don't ever become aware of what's going on with themselves and can't rise above. You can be self-aware or be a victim.

When it comes to stress, there is no avoiding it. How you deal with it, however, is your decision to make. Go ahead and throw an epic toddler tantrum, scream into a pillow, angry run, kickbox, but find a healthy way to manage your stress, not an unhealthy way to deal with it. If you've tried every healthy outlet to destress, and it's not working, go to a therapist. There's no shame in it, especially if it helps you become aware while also helping you avoid turning to unhealthy options. Short-term unhealthy fixes will only lead to situations that cause you more stress down the road so don't be counterproductive and figure out what healthy method works best for you.

Chapter 7:

Go for the Gold Medal in Healthy Living

SHE SAID

I'm a huge cheerleader for living a healthy lifestyle of exercise, diet, and good mental health. While I wasn't always as disciplined as I am now, the healthy lifestyle I lead is worth the sacrifice and commitment because of the benefits. A healthy diet gives you the fuel to maintain physical health, and good physical health will boost your mental health. Most of us don't realize how important our health is until we are not healthy. I think it's imperative to try proactively to suck less at healthy living so that we can avoid learning by making mistakes with our health.

Exercise

To some people's ears, the word "exercise" is more offensive than a cuss word. Just say the word to them and watch their reactions. I'm not sure why so many adults are so averse to exercise, but it's something more people could use more of. I am a daily exerciser who is always looking for more ways to get bonus exercise throughout my day.

I remember back to 2008 in the early years of my first marriage when I hadn't yet found the motivation to exercise regularly. I did a lot of sitting for work and a lot of eating three meals a day, and slowly my weight started to creep up and up. Laziness breeds more laziness, and it took a moderately traumatic incident for me to realize that I needed to start exercising. That and I looked at some photos of myself, and I don't think that the camera adds fifteen pounds. That weight was on me, literally.

Regardless of what prompts or motivates you to exercise, the benefits will make the effort worth it. Daily exercise gives me more energy in my day, my clothes fit better, and I feel pretty great. On the very infrequent days that I take a day off, I find myself sluggish, and unmotivated, and I snack more. No, adding a little exercise into your life does NOT give you the license to eat more, like how some women think being pregnant means eating for two instead of 1.1. That's not how food math works: don't buy into that logic… it's all lies!

When I started running on a treadmill, I would watch how many calories I burned, and when I realized that a mile on the treadmill only burned 200 calories which is a can of regular pop, that was an eye-opener. No, I don't count calories on the regular, but having a rough idea of how much effort you have to put in to burn off something that can so easily be replaced will help you see food in a different way.

> *Jane's friend and coworker Sandy had just been to the doctor for her annual checkup, and her doctor informed her that her blood pressure was high and that she was pre-diabatic. "Can you believe this*

BS!? I'm only forty-one," she complained to Jane the day after she visited the doctor.

"Well Sandy, I mean, I love you so don't take this the wrong way, but ever since you moved in with Alan, you've kind of… gotten comfortable," she said with trepidation.

"Did you just call me fat?!" she snapped at Jane. *"Well, not exactly, but I think your body and your doctor might be trying to tell you that you need to make some changes."*

"So, I'm fat?" Sandy asked again.

"Just stop it. I want you to be healthy for you and your family." Jane said with sincerity. *"Don't you want to make sure that you're around to see your boys grow up and have families of their own?"* she continued.

"Yeah, I suppose I should think about changing some things up. What treadmill do you have, and do you like it?" she asked Jane.

"I just love it. Joy and I both do. I'll send you the information when I get home," Jane said. "You know, Sandy, in the interim between now and when you decide on a treadmill, you can go out for walks with your dog before and after work," she suggested.

"That's actually a really good idea. Maybe I can get up a little earlier to take the dog out. Thanks for being such a good friend, for calling me out and telling me the truth," Sandy said as she got up to hug Jane.

Sometimes it takes a traumatic event or some scary news from the doctor to motivate us to want to make a change to the lifestyle we have settled into and become comfortable in. The key is to maintain what works when you find it, and don't make excuses for why you can't continue it. Even if you have thirty minutes at the end of your day where you find yourself on social media or binge-watching a show, you can either do that while on a piece of exercise equipment, or you can shift that time to a healthier pastime.

Here are a few ways that you can start to take baby steps into exercise while you're finding something a bit more intense and regular:

1. Take the stairs instead of an elevator or escalator or run up and down the stairs a few times during the day like I do if I eat a donut.
2. Walk to a co-worker's office instead of emailing or messaging them.
3. Take a short walk after you eat lunch, even if it's just around the parking lot.
4. Do some wall sits when you are in your friend's office for a chit-chat (I do this, but people in my office know I'm weird already).
5. Get a standing desk or an under-desk elliptical.
6. Take a walk with your family after dinner.
7. Do sit-ups during commercial breaks when you're watching TV.

I heard somewhere that the best time of the day to exercise is first thing in the morning. That's great for a morning person like me. I spring out of bed and am on the treadmill around 4:30 am. I also heard somewhere that you should think of exercise like showering… it's something that simply becomes part of your daily routine and can't be skipped. My OBGYN told me after my first child was born that there were three ways to shed pregnancy hormones: pee them out, cry them out, or sweat them out. I think I cried a lot of them out, but sweating is great for your pores and your skin… force all that crap out of your skin and out of your body! If you think popping a pimple is satisfying, think about how satisfying a whole-body pop would feel as you sweat out the toxins.

Diet

While exercise is a key ingredient to a healthy lifestyle, food is also equally as important. Fad diets, miracle drinks, and any new-age pills on the market are not healthy lifestyle options. They are short-term solutions that will often end and leave you right back where you started. Healthy living is simple: Diet and exercise. It's not like this secret has been recently discovered in some tablet etching from before the dawn of time.

There are no quick fixes. If there was, we'd all be doing it. Duh. Here are some ways to start yourself on a healthier path:

1. Replace a carb side with a side of fruit or vegetables with meals.
2. Make as many meals from scratch as you can to avoid the preservatives and unknowns in processed ingredients.
3. Eat more protein and less carbs.
4. When you are feeling hungry, drink a glass of water.
5. Cut the sugar intake. Sugar hides in many foods that you wouldn't expect.
6. Snack healthy: nuts, fruit, cheese, & carrot sticks (without the ranch dressing).
7. Substitute regular pop for diet, but flavored water is even better. Anything with carbonation will eat away at your tooth enamel so unless you plan to dress up in the future for Halloween as a Jack-O-Lantern, choose water.

Being able to switch your mindset to seeing food as fuel, at least some of the time, will help you to see it differently. Most restaurants print calories on their menus, so it's easier to shop for healthier options. If you view food as putting the right kind of gas in your car, it will put you in more of a "fill the hole" mindset instead of viewing food as a coping mechanism, an impulse craving satisfier, or even something to do out of boredom.

If you know when your weak times of the day are, make sure that you have healthier options ready and available. If you know you get munchies for snacks at 7:00 pm as I do, but you didn't peel and cut the carrots into sticks, you're certainly not going to do the prep work when your body is tired and craving comfort foods.

I like to take an apple to work with me along with a sharp knife, and I keep paper plates in my office because I know I will only eat apples if they're cut up. There are also pistachios and dried mangoes in my office for when I get the munchies, and someone brings in donuts… again. I mean, there are so many donuts that come into my office that it's almost become routine to "Just say no" every morning.

Luckily for me, I have found a few other ways to avoid these tasty donuts. One of my friends who sees me heading for the bakery boxes quickly says, "I spit in them!" because she knows how real my struggle with pastries is. Sometimes I also lean over with my nose next to the box, open it, and flap it up and down while taking a big inhale of the sweet sugar into my nose. Yes, my coworkers think I'm weird, and one of them keeps telling me about the Emily program for eating disorders, but hey, we all do what we gotta do.

Do I ever treat myself to treats? Um, yeah! I'm not an alien robot. If you don't allow yourself to have the things you love every now and then, you'll freak out and have a meltdown. I spend a lot of my summer days in the drive though at the Dairy Queen, waiting for my favorite seasonal Blizzard. Sometimes I find myself with the largest lunch order at work lunches... "I'll have the tremendous twelve with a side of French Silk pie, please." People are horrified at how much food I can consume in one sitting.

One of my favorite indulgences was Wavy Lays. Every night, I would find myself magically on the couch with a bowl of greasy chips in my lap. How did that get there??? After a while, I realized that my morning headaches were caused by the amount of salt I was taking in at night, so I reluctantly gave up one of my vices.

A few weekends ago, I took my boys to my parents' house to celebrate Easter, and my mom had chips out for lunch. "I don't remember the last time I had chips," I commented as I loaded half my plate up with the salty goodness. A few days later, I found myself at the store with a bag of Wavy Lays in my shopping cart. 'Ooh old friend, we meet again,' I thought as I planned out my evening snack. As that bowl of greasy chips settled back into the place it remembered as home, I was excited to experience the salty, greasy crunch again.

"Ugh!" I said out loud to myself. Yeah, I talk to myself a lot. I've heard that talking to yourself is a sign of genius. At least that's what I tell myself when I'm talking to myself. Regardless, the salty memory was better than the treat I was having. Did they change the recipe? I couldn't even finish half the bowl. I mean, I even got up off the couch and put the rest back into the bag. Who was I?

What had changed was that my body had gotten used to the salt intake and craved it, but after I had broken the cycle, I couldn't go back. Think of it like being infatuated with someone for a long time, then realizing they're a terrible person and are bad for you, and then you can't see them the same way again… Chips… I'm breaking up with you for good! It's not you, it's me… well, maybe it is you. I loved you SO much, but we had a toxic relationship, and I can't see you anymore! Farewell, and I wish you the best.

HE SAID

She: When did you start exercising, and why did you start?

He: I started primarily when I got into wrestling when I was in sixth or seventh grade.

She: Seriously?

He: Yep, I got one of those crappy concrete weight benches in the basement, and my dad made me some bars down at work. But I ended up bending those because I put too much weight on them.

She: *(Giggling)* Of course you did.

He: That's where I started, and I've been doing it ever since.

She: What has kept you doing it for fifty years?

He: I like the way it makes me look, and I don't like feeling weak. I like my body to be hard, and I want to feel like I have the ability to protect myself and the ones around me. I also like the way it feels to push my body.

She: So, is that what keeps you motivated to work out every day?

He: Yeah, I don't want to lose that. I know I'll lose it eventually, but I want to prolong it as long as I can. It's a big part of how I see myself and the value I have in myself.

She: But you told me a while ago that you used to think that your drive to stay in shape was internal until you got married and realized maybe it was more for getting women.

He: Yeah, and being intimidating to people, but the results feel good too.

She: Remember that slump where you got a little softer and weaker? What happened there?

He: I was comfortable, but I think the thing that snapped me out of that funk and motivated me was your first book's cover photoshoot.

She: *(Bursts out laughing)* Hahaha!

He: I looked at it after you edited it and thought, "That doesn't look like me. Now people are going to have an expectation of what I look like so now I'm going to have to push harder."

She: *(Still laughing hysterically)* So, your internal motivation now more recently is because I Photoshopped you a little on the cover of a book?

He: Yeah.

She: That's funny. How can other people find their OWN motivation when they're an adult and they need to make some healthy changes?

He: You have to become very self-aware about what is important to you because many times people don't know what's important to them. They're just unhappy, but they don't know why they're unhappy, and they don't know what would make them happy. Without those pieces, you aren't going to have any motivation. You have to have a purpose and see where it can lead you.

That's why books like this self-help book exist. People go out and look for answers. "These people seem happy, what are they doing to make themselves happy?" you reach out and start looking for success that you can apply to your life.

Most people don't get better without someone from the outside bringing a new perspective. That's where it's also important to have friend groups like we talked about before… people you trust. Those are the people who can come in and assist you when you don't know what to do.

She: But it's not their job to push you.

He: No, but sometimes it takes someone you respect to come in and support you. When I used to assist people in personal training, I would tell them to keep their goals in retrospect of what is doable. Don't have huge goals. Focus on what you get out of it when you start and build on that momentum of progress. In other words, get up and do something, and keep doing it until it gets easier, then push yourself harder. You need to replace negative energy with positive energy.

She: I'm shifting the conversation. What has been the hardest food you've had to give up?

He: Candy.

She: Why did you give it up?

He: When you discipline yourself to sacrifice something you love more than anything, that's the hardest thing to do. But it's also the most rewarding thing to do because you show that you have control over yourself and your situation because you can go without. Pretty soon, you don't crave it as badly.

She: But why did you give it up?

He: Because I could see that all I wanted to do was eat candy, and it wasn't healthy. It didn't make me feel good after I ate it.

She: How do you feel now that you've not had it in years?

He: I don't miss it, really.

She: Do you feel healthier?

He: Oh yeah, way better. I used to get so high off of it that it would give me mood changes. I would almost get crabby when I couldn't have it.

She: Like an addiction.

He: Yes. It was all I wanted.

She: But didn't you say something like on your death bed you want all the candy?

He: Yeah, but I don't even know if that's true anymore. I would love to eat it, but I know if I do, I'll go right down the spiral.

She: So, you are saying that on some level, there's a lot of power in denying yourself something that you want.

He: Oh, absolutely. There's tons of power there, and that flows into other things you are doing. If I have the power to deny myself something that I really want and really like, then I've gotta have the power to achieve something that's hard to do, or I have the power to change my life for the better. Self-motivation is important.

When it comes to changing habits and living a healthier lifestyle, stop making excuses. Don't even open your mouth to do it. There is always something that you can do, there is always a way to make time, and there is always going to be a benefit.

I always have candy and sweets around, but most times I don't eat them. People used to ask me how I could avoid it, and I always said that if it's around, I can avoid it, but if it's not, I crave it. Maybe it was my subconscious trying to desensitize me to candy. If you see it all the time and can ignore it and train yourself not to want it, it becomes easier to avoid.

Living a healthy lifestyle starts with a mindset shift. Finding your internal self-motivation is the most crucial factor. Once you find that, the rest will fall into place because you will be determined to make all the right changes for the right reasons. After you start to experience the benefits, those benefits will drive you to keep at it and push yourself harder, and the healthy cycle and benefits will perpetuate.

Chapter 8:

"Sweatpants" Is My Safe Word

SHE SAID

I'm not confirming or denying anything, but let's just say that if I had a safe word, it would be "sweatpants". Why? Because I don't own any, I've never owned any, and I will never own any so that makes the likelihood of my saying it in casual conversation in or out of the bedroom pretty slim. The very utterance of the word sends an icy chill down my spine like the name "Mufasa" did to the hyenas in the original animated Disney movie *The Lion King*.

Me: I just hear that word and I shudder.

You: Sweatpants.

Me: Ooh. Do it again.

You: Sweatpants.

Me: OOOOHHH…

You: SWEATPANTS, SWEATPANTS, SWEATPANTS!

My version of a horror film would be one where everyone in every role wore sweatpants and thought it was acceptable: doctors, lawyers, beauty queens. The fashion police have either significantly relaxed their statutes or have been disbanded. The only time that sweatpants should be acceptable to be worn in public is over shorts to and from the gym or a sport, running outside, or coming home from the hospital after major surgery.

Ooh, and let's address sweatpants' slightly less ugly sister, leggings. I'm not a fan of leggings in 90% of instances that I see them being worn. I'm sorry, but I don't want to be able to know what furniture you sat on last because I can see the detailed imprint of said furniture left on your rear. It's inappropriate. Leggings under a dress, okay, maybe if you're a freeze baby like one of my friends is, but leggings, where your whole ass is showing, are just wrong. It burns the eyes of onlookers who unknowingly stare into the sun, like looking at an eclipse as the moon slowly moves to reveal the too bright light. AAHHH!!! My eyes!

Maybe there should be leggings glasses like eclipse glasses! You could wear the glasses when you leave the house just in case you end up eye to ass with a full moon legging eclipse. Lucky wearers of these special glasses would see someone with normal pants on and would be spared the trauma and permanent retina damage.

If you're reading this book and are wearing sweatpants, I sure hope you're at home or the gym. If you're wearing leggings, please cover your butt. If you are a sweatpants or leggings frequent offender, you may need to think about sucking less at style and fashion. It is my observation that any semblance of elegance has almost been irradicated from most people's daily fashion and style. People used to dress in slacks and button-down shirts or dresses with heels. Now it's commonplace to see someone and have no idea if they're sleepwalking in their pajamas and Crocs or if they're a zombie.

The last style pet peeve I have are Birkenstocks, or what I call "Jesus shoes". Birks are ambiguous footwear that I find extremely unappealing to the eye. What were the designers thinking? "Hey, let's make a sandal that isn't masculine or feminine, makes your foot look twice as big and flat, and resembles something a caveman might have fashioned for himself using primitive tools." There's a running joke in my office about these sandals. Everyone knows my extreme aversion to them as a fashion statement. The worst, and they know this, is when they wear leggings with socks and Birkenstocks. Kill me now.

Oh, and you'd think that the retailers that have my email subscriptions would know my shopping habits better than most, but I get solicitations from my favorite retailers promoting Birkenstocks. To ME! Do they not know me at all?

I thought AI, Alexa, and my phone were listening to me to provide me with tailored ads to con me out of my money. I guess technology isn't as advanced as I thought.

But COVID-19... made us all so comfortable. No, no. That's an excuse. Fashion and personal style were headed into the crapper way before that. But why? What happened, and how can we bring a little bit of elegance back to everyday fashion, or is all hope lost?

> Dick had taken on a project at work that allowed him to work from home for several months. While his being at home was great for shuttling Joy around to school activities, it was not great for his personal appearance. The man who used to leave the house clean-shaven and with a crisp suit on was now looking more like a sasquatch than the clean-cut man Jane had married.
>
> "Dick..." Jane started. "I love you, but just because you're home all day, I don't think that you should wear your pajamas all day." Hearing the sound of her husband's sloppy house slippers that foreshadowed his appearance in pajama pants was

starting to make her want to smack the unwelcomed new beard right off his face.

"Why? I'm not going anywhere." Dick countered.

"Well, because I have to look at you, and I don't find this new look particularly attractive," she explained in a way so as not to be ambiguous to his logical man brain.

"I see. Well, don't sugarcoat it for my benefit," he said with a chuckle.

"I'm serious, Dick. Maybe we should use this opportunity to make some overall changes to your wardrobe. I think that you can be comfortable at home in clothes that are a little less appalling," she compromised. "I mean, if you want me to want to have sex with you, you might want to be a little more appealing to your target audience," she continued.

"Since we are on the subject of style dear, maybe you could get some outfits that highlight your assets more," Dick said with a wink. "Oh, Dick, you're terrible! But if that's my okay to get new

clothes, I'll get some more tailored clothes," she said as she mentally planned their next shopping trip.

I remember when my grandmother would get dressed to go out, even to the grocery store. She put on a dress, heels, and jewelry. She never went out without her hair done and looking her best. I always aspire to look my best when I leave the house for a multitude of reasons: I feel more confident and myself when I look put together, I enjoy putting outfits together, I think that clothes should be worn and not left to rot on a hanger waiting for the perfect occasion, and I feel like proper attire should be worn when leaving the house.

Several of my coworkers in separate instances have sent me the same exact meme with the photo of Glenda the Good Witch in her poufy pink ball gown, crown, and wand with the overlay of this text:

> Work: You have to dress for the job you want, not the job you have.

> Me: *arrives at work* (*dressed as a fairy princess, essentially*).

The funny thing is that to some degree, they're not wrong. I did find a way to dress like a queen with a crown and everything for work one Christmas season. It was kind of awesome. So, in that regard, I have lived and enjoyed this meme to its fullest.

How do you make a statement about the sense of fashion in the office without saying something about the fashion in the office? Here's how: Just the other day, a coworker and I came in wearing very similar outfits. "We're twins!" I pointed out.

"We're twins, but I'm the basic b*tch version, and I'm okay with that," she said as we all laughed. That same coworker wanted to take a selfie with my work wife the next day and said to her, "Make sure you look cute tomorrow!" I mean… she said it, I didn't.

While it's a bit tongue in cheek that I lived out my princess fantasy, there is a lot of truth to dressing for the job you want, or at a minimum, dressing like you give a damn. Being well put together shows that you are confident and that you have your sh*t together, and most people will treat you better if you are dressed for respect.

If you respect yourself enough to put in effort, others will notice and will treat you with a higher level of respect. If you don't believe me, give it a try. Elevate your style for a week and go about your normal routine. See how differently people treat you, how differently you feel, and I will have made my point.

I understand that I am a bit on the extreme side of attire with my collection of stilettos for every occasion and season, and a jewelry armoire filled with statement jewelry, but if you want to up your game a little bit and suck less at style, try some of these tips:

1. Wear heels with jeans (stilettos can be worked up to from wedges, block heels, or kitten heels).
2. Change your crew-neck t-shirts out for dressier or fitted shirts with more flattering necklines.

3. Dress up your casual outfits with statement earrings or necklaces.
4. Add a few skirts and dresses to your outfit rotation (dresses can be so much more comfortable than sweatpants or leggings).
5. Add color to your wardrobe. Figure out what colors look best on you, and please get some.
6. Find out how to dress to flatter your figure and start converting your wardrobe.
7. Do your hair and makeup every day.

Yes, it's true. I have been heard saying things like, "If you're not uncomfortable, you're just not trying hard enough", and "You haven't lived if you haven't bled into a pair of heels," but hey, those phrases are just my way of adding shock value to the point I'm trying to make about sucking less at style… and yes, I have bled in heels, and I'm always a little uncomfortable.

HE SAID

She: How would you describe your sense of fashion or style?

He: Aahhhh… crappy.

She: I'm serious.

He: I'm serious too.

She: You don't feel like you have any fashion or style or anything?

He: Other than what you brought into my life? Before you, it was like biker bar t-shirts and jeans.

She: How would you describe my sense of fashion or style?

He: Uh, what's the word I'm looking for?

She: Be nice…

He: Upscale, but I think you've got your own thing going on.

She: That's not very descriptive.

He: It's like kind of boo-GEE... booshy...

She: *(Laughing at his attempts to pronounce it).* Bougie. What do you think about how people today dress in everyday life?

He: I think you feel how you dress. It shows a mindset.

She: I'm talking about people in general and how they leave the house.

He: Society has changed over the years. When President Regan was in office, he never ever would be seen in the Oval Office without a tie on because it showed respect and professionalism, but now we have presidents who don't wear ties.

She: But I'm talking about regular people.

He: But it shows how society has gone down and is nonprofessional. People used to go to church and dress up. If you look at pictures from the 20's, people had ties and hats, and no one does that anymore. People don't tie how they dress to the character they are trying to portray.

She: Why has it become okay for people to wear pajamas and Crocks out in public?

He: Because it's acceptable and is the societal trend. There has been a downshift in professionalism and how you look in public. It's a cultural shift.

She: Didn't you say once that you'd love to have a life where you could wear an expensive suit every day?

He: Yeah, I think that'd be cool.

She: Why did you say that?

He: Because I think it makes you feel good to be dressed up. You have more confidence when you dress a certain way.

She: So, you, in theory, would like to go the opposite way than society?

He: Yeah, I think it's nice, but I still like to be comfortable. It's not like I want to go fishing in a suit or go to the gym wearing a suit.

She: Be serious. What do you think of leggings being worn in public?

He: Are you talking about stretchy pants?

She: Yes.

He: I think that certain people shouldn't wear certain things.

She: But they're not pants.

He: If they look good on you, I'm fine with them and looking at shapely bodies in stretchy pants, but I'm not fine with seeing spongey donut sacks with ricotta cheese pushed into sandwich bags. That's gross.

She: Did my personal style or fashion sense have any influence on why you were attracted to me?

He: Yes and no. It makes me look better.

She: I mean like why you decided to go out with me initially.

He: No because those pictures didn't mean anything. I didn't know you dressed like that all the time. I didn't realize that until spending some time with you and that you dressed like that every day. Most people change. In the wintertime, I would have expected you to dress down a little bit, but nope, that didn't happen. I'm fine with it, but I had to up my game.

She: What do you think men and women should dress like and why?

He: Culturally, I don't see a problem with how people dress.

She: There are no standards, though.

He: But that's the way culture has gone. There's no pressure to be better. I'm conservative so I think people should dress appropriately for the situation. There is less inspiration these days for people to better themselves, but you should dress for what you want to be.

I understand that there is a middle ground between business formal and sweatpants, and if you can find a style between those extremes, you're likely doing better than most. If you are, however, looking to elevate your style to push you ahead in your life, try putting more effort in. If you can learn to manage your time more effectively in the morning, you can use the extra time to do your hair and makeup, iron your outfits, and accessorize.

Even my time-management-challenged husband takes the time to polish his shoes before we go out. "What are you wearing?" he asked one time before we went out together. "Why?" I ask. "Because I don't want to look like a slouch next to you." He responded. There you have it. Try not to look like a slouch and elevate your style.

Chapter 9:

Girl Math Won't Help You Retire Early

SHE SAID

Oh boy was I the queen of girl math. I used to rationalize all the time to my first husband about how spending more to save more made sense every time a coupon arrived in the mail from one of my shopping Achilles heel retailers. "But if I spend $150, I'll get $30 off instead of getting only $20 off $100," I would rationalize with my girl math. "But you're still spending more money in the end though," he would counter. "But I neeeeed it."

Not only was I great at combining girl math logic with whining, but I always seemed to manage to get my ex into a store because they were having a sale. The problem is that I'm like a truffle pig who can sniff out the one item NOT for sale during a store-wide sale, and that's the only item I want. I have expensive taste, what can I say? It's a gift.

The retailers had me tricked and trained into their discount logic. Ironically, in the two above scenarios, they both equate to 20% off, but the way they market it pushes you to spend more than if they'd just said there was a 20% off storewide sale. Smart… But now I'm smarter.

Part of me misses the carefree frivolity of my retail cycle of shame: the high of spending followed by wallowing in buyer's remorse followed by retail therapy spending, and so on. However, using your pink girl math calculator and burying your head in the sand when it comes to managing your money as an adult will leave you destitute and on the street when you're in your golden years or are in some sort of county assistance program with the bare minimum of care. Don't think it can't happen. I work at a non-profit that offers social services so I know how bad it can get, and it's not a place you ever want to find yourself.

Sigh. Adulting takes the fun out of everything, doesn't it? Except The Boobie Cup. Regardless of if you have a partner who has a good retirement plan, you should still have a base knowledge of money management for several reasons. Something may happen, and you may not always be with that partner, and you shouldn't assume that your partner has the finances under control and set up for retirement.

Honesty, I wish someone had educated me sooner about saving for retirement and money management. Oh, wait! My dad did. For years… like every time I saw him or talked to him on the phone, and I hated it. Thank goodness he never gave up on me because I finally found the motivation to figure it out and have begun to take it very seriously. So seriously, that I'm now reciting to my friends the same lines that used to irritate me when said by my father. "But what about your retirement!?" I say as I try to convince them to set themselves up for a successful future.

The me that used to impulse buy everything because I'd convinced myself I "needed" it now says things like, "If it's not gas or groceries, I'm not buying it." The girl who bought the same shirt in every color because it was efficient now says, "I don't need more clothes; my closets are full anyway." Who have I become? I hardly recognize myself... even though I should very easily recognize myself, considering I'm wearing old clothes I've had for years because I'm making smart financial decisions!

It's not funny, but it kind of is, but it's not. Money apparently does NOT grow on trees, unfortunately, and it's certainly not a fun thing to think, learn, or talk about. But adulting isn't always fun and sometimes requires a level of responsibility.

Let's start with budgeting. Ugh. That word. Budget. I used to HATE it so much. If I heard "budget" or the word "retirement", I would find ways to change the subject as quickly as possible. "Danger, DANGER! Abort! Run away!"

However, when you become a single parent of two who's on her own, you have no choice but to turn to budgeting so that you can make sure that you aren't living paycheck-to-paycheck. Yes, I like to learn my lessons the hard way, but most people don't just learn to do something they've been avoiding their whole lives for no reason.

The way I like to stay on budget is by anal retentively entering all my expenditures into a spreadsheet. I need that sign that says, "I have a spreadsheet for that," because it's kind of true. Years back I created a budget spreadsheet that breaks down fixed monthly expenses and adds them up, subtracts them from my monthly income, and then breaks down the remaining money into subcategories that each has a mini-budget of their own… or sub-budgets. Is that a thing? Well, it is now.

The variable expenses get deducted from the remaining funds (minus fixed expenses), and with every purchase, I know how much I have left to spend. I don't expect most people to log every expense like I do, but it's a system that helps keep me in check.

Some people use debit cards instead of credit cards because "then I know how much money I have left in my account". Okay, well, that's not the smartest option. Why?

1. You are missing out on FREE rewards from credit card companies.
2. You are missing out on building credit by using a credit card and paying it off every month.
3. Credit cards are more secure than debit cards because they can help protect you against fraudulent purchases.

Credit cards are not the Devil. You simply need to be a responsible user of them, and you can reap the rewards. Literally! I have paid for hotel stays with FREE points, round trip international airline tickets with points, and I get money back on other cards. Never have I had to carry a balance and pay the exorbitant interest rate that the credit card companies hope you'll need to pay. Haha... joke's on you.

Whether you are single or have a partner, you should both understand what's coming in, what's going out, what should be saved, and where there is wiggle room. Money is one of the big three things couples fight about, and there's a good reason for that. One person may feel like they're bringing more to the table so they think they can spend more, and the other person feels like that's not fair logic. Sometimes one person handles the money, the other person spends it without knowledge of the financial parameters and overspends, causing a fight. Money is a big deal but requires effective communication, mutual respect, and understanding.

If you need to sit down with a pencil and paper or a spreadsheet of your very own, you should be taking money management seriously so that you don't lose sleep at night wondering how you'll be able to pay all the bills.

After you've assessed your financial situation, you can focus on planning for retirement. I mean, I seriously cannot believe these words are coming out of my fingers. My dad would be SO proud!

With a serious face and in my dad-impression voice, "You need to pay yourself first." What does that mean? It means that you shouldn't do your budget and look at what's left to see what you can "pay yourself" with. Budget your retirement investment money into the recurring monthly expenses, not into the area where you allocate extra funds.

Paying yourself first is essentially the 401(k) model of retirement saving. The company takes a percentage of your paycheck pre-tax and pre-you, and they put it into your retirement investment account. Your retirement account is what WILL pay you when you retire. If you have an individual retirement account, or IRA, then you need to set aside money to invest before you look at how much extra you have to spend on non-essentials.

Let's start with company matching because it's a no-brainer. If your company matches up to a certain percentage, always contribute the max that they will match. Always. It's FREE money! Free. Take it.

No matter what point you are at in your life (unless you're retired), you can still invest toward your future. Ideally, you would start investing as early as humanly possible into an IRA until a company match or pension presents itself, but even then, you should diversify and invest in your IRA as well as your company match. Just start as early as you can because the early bird gets the retirement nest egg. Chirp'n A.

I am by no means a financial advisor, but if this was a book written about financial advice from a financial advisor, you'd likely be asleep by now. However, please feel free to fact-check me with an actual financial advisor or Google, if you prefer, because I'm not an expert.

In my experience, there are two different forms of personal retirement account investment options: Traditional IRAs and ROTH IRAs. You can put your post-tax money from your in-pocket paycheck into both accounts. The difference is that with a Traditional IRA, you will get a tax break on it because it's a pre-tax account that you've paid the tax on.

Traditional IRA

You get paid with taxes taken out -> you invest in a Traditional IRA -> government gives the IRA contribution taxes back –> you pay taxes on the money when you withdraw at retirement.

If you want to roll over an old 401(k), you can roll it over into your Traditional IRA because a 401(k) is a pre-tax investment account as well. Pre-tax goes to pre-tax pretty seamlessly… I mean, if you can manage to understand and get right the paperwork involved. Get the Advil bottle; you're gonna need it. I did. You can roll over your 401(k) into a Roth, but "since you haven't paid income taxes on that money in your traditional 401(k) account, you will owe taxes on the money for the year when you roll it over into a Roth IRA" (Investopedia.com; Must-Know Rules for Converting Your 401(k) to a Roth IRA).

I know it's a lot but stay with me. When you start drawing on your Roth IRA at age 59 ½ (or later) you won't have to pay tax on them because you already paid taxes on the money before you invested it. This option is good if you want to avoid paying a higher income tax rate in the future. The downside is that there isn't a tax deduction on your annual contributions like there is with a Traditional IRA.

Roth IRA

You get paid with taxes taken out -> you invest in a Roth IRA -> you don't pay taxes when you withdraw at retirement because you already paid taxes that were not paid back by the government

If you're looking to invest while also enjoying a tax deduction annually or are looking to roll over a Traditional 401(k) without having to pay taxes, then a Traditional IRA is a good way for you to save. These IRAs are tax-deferred so you don't have to pay tax on the money until you make withdrawals at or after the age of 59 ½.

In both instances, you'll have money later, but whether you'll have to pay taxes on that money now or later is up to you. With both IRAs (as of this year, 2024) you can contribute $7,000 per year. If you are over the age of 50, you can contribute $8,000 a year to help you catch up on retirement investing.

Dick and Jane had not been actively managing their money because they figured they had time. Instead of investing in their future, the pair had been buying "toys" in the form of a boat, a third car and big vacations. Well, they did have time, but now they were getting older, and they were verging on it being too late to reap the benefits of long-game retirement investing.

At the age of 49, Dick had a wake-up call moment when some of his older friends were retiring early. They were talking about being able to buy and enjoy the things that Dick had spent his money on before saving for retirement, and he started to wonder if he would even be able to retire.

"Jane, I think we're in trouble," said as he rushed in the door at the end of the workday.

"Why, Dick? What's wrong?" she asked with growing concern.

"Some of my friends are retiring early, and I think we need to look at our options for retirement," he explained.

"Oh. How bad is it?" she asked.

"I don't know. I made an appointment with a financial advisor, but we are going to have to make some serious changes to our spending."

"But I like our lifestyle," Jane countered.

"I understand that, Jane, but would you rather have all the things now, and have to work until we die, or would you rather be able to retire… eventually, and still be able to have fun then too?" he asked.

After their appointment with the financial advisor, Dick rolled over an old 401(k) into a Traditional IRA, they sold their boat, and maxed out their annual contribution with the sale. "Jane, I think that if we scale back our vacations and maybe take them every other year, we can make bigger contributions to our retirement, especially since

I'll be able to contribute more next year after I turn 50."

"I'd better talk to my HR department and see what I can do on my side too," said Jane. After speaking with HR, Jane was excited to share her progress and contribution to the retirement pot with Dick. "So, I realized that I was only contributing 3% of my salary to my 401(k) at work, but the company matches up to 6% so I changed my pre-tax contributions to 6%!" she said in a giddy voice.

"That's great, dear. I think if we can cut back and max out personal and work contributions, we might not be able to retire early, but we will be able to retire. Maybe we should start a Roth IRA too and contribute there as well," he mused.

"I'm on board. We can cut back and still do the things we enjoy. I love you, Dick."

"Love you too, honey."

But what about that person who never spent any money, saved it all to retire, and then died before retirement? Okay, don't be dramatic. While I certainly advocate for maxing out your retirement contributions to your company match and at least one IRA, I'm not suggesting that you don't enjoy your life before retirement.

I remember eavesdropping on one of my hubby's conversations with his 95-year-old grandfather. His wife of almost seventy years of marriage passed away during the COVID-19 pandemic, and he has been a bit lost and lonely ever since. During the conversation where Andy was filling in his grandpa about our plans, he mentioned that we were looking forward to our vacation to the Bahamas. "That's great! Good for you! You should be taking trips and enjoying your life," he cheered.

He and his wife had enjoyed so many trips, and he has the photo albums to prove it. I know how much they meant to him because I've heard the stories, and I want to have those memories and stories too when I'm at a point where I cannot travel. My point is that you can do both: save for retirement but also enjoy the people in your life in the present. All you need to do is suck less at money management.

HE SAID

He: *(As the conversation from the last chapter flows into this interview)* I don't have your mindset for this. You're expecting me to know automatically what you want me to say…

She: I'm expecting you to… be better.

He: *(Laughs)*

She: So, suck less at answering my questions. Do you know what "girl math" is?

He: Yes, I do.

She: What is it?

He: Girl math is making things line up and look a certain way to benefit the way that women think, which is not practical and rational. It's emotional and touchy-feely.

She: Do you think that you're good at managing your money?

He: Ah, no.

She: *(Laughs)* What do you do well to manage your money effectively?

He: Not have any of it.

She: What could you improve on when it comes to money management?

He: Planning ahead.

She: Planning ahead how?

He: By buying food and stuff to have on hand so I'm not stopping at the gas stations for impulse buys.

She: What systems do you use to make sure you are saving enough and are controlling spending?

He: I put money in my deferred comp and into my savings account every paycheck.

She: What about controlling spending? What systems are you putting into place to make sure you aren't overspending?

He: I make sure my credit card is always paid off so I'm not paying interest, I don't buy things I can't afford, and I fix a lot of stuff on my own, so I don't have to pay someone to do it.

She: Okay. Do you think that you've done a good job planning for your retirement?

He: No. It could be better.

She: Is there anything you wish you would have done differently or sooner, and why?

He: Yeah, I wish I would have put more into my deferred comp from the beginning, I wish I would have bought my military time back in the beginning, I wish I wouldn't have gone through a divorce, and I wish that I wouldn't have wrecked every car I've had since I was a kid.

She: How did the divorce affect your retirement?

He: It didn't affect my retirement, but it set me back financially to where I was scraping by for a long time and had to pay back a lot of crap that I incurred then. You can't save for the future when you're frickin' pinching pennies to survive. I wouldn't have had to do that if I'd made better life choices with a better partner who was more responsible and could be an equal player. I wouldn't have had to pay for attorneys…

She: What is your shopping Achilles heel, and do you think it's a smart way to spend your money?

He: Shopping Achilles heel… *(Makes a duck face with his lips as he thinks)*

She: It should not be a hard question.

He: Shopping Achilles heel…

She: Really?

He: What is my shopping Achilles heel?

She: Weapons?

He: But I buy and sell them.

She: That's a pretty big Achilles heel!

He: But I don't get stuff that I can't get rid of and make a similar amount of money back.

She: So, you're buying it thinking that you're going to sell it later for essentially the same price plus inflation. If you hadn't spent that money in the first place, you could have invested it somewhere where it could have been earning interest.

He: Yeah, but I could have also spent it on something else that was frivolous, that didn't maintain value.

She: So, your knife collecting is just a savings account with no interest, is that what you're saying?

He: Or it's just something to do. It pleasures me. What else are you going to do with your money? Gotta be happy somehow.

She: *(Sighs with frustration)* Don't you ever have buyer's remorse with those?

He: Oh yeah, with just about everything. There's nothing that I buy that I don't feel bad about after.

She: Except for my wedding rings?

He: Yasss… there you go.

One of my good friends was explaining to me about her favorite kind of earrings and how she gets these handmade pieces for "a good deal" because her friend gives her a discount. "That's girl math," I told her because she's still spending money on something superfluous because she's convinced herself it's such a good deal, that it cannot be passed up.

Money now, or money later? That is the question. Wouldn't it be great if we could just tell the future and know what we would need to do or not do financially to live our whole lives to their fullest? Well, we can't so that means we have to do our best with the knowledge that we have.

Count yourself lucky for the people who love you and who nag at you to be better or do better. They aren't doing it because it's fun for them to see you squirm. Okay, maybe a sibling might, but people who truly love you want the best for you now and in the future. Heed their advice, no matter how it is delivered, and you'll thank them later for giving you the tough love you needed to suck less.

Chapter 10:

Meal Planning for Those Who Hate the Grocery Store

SHE SAID

What did the grocery store ever do to me? Nothing really. My parents owned a grocery store/gas station for twenty-five years, and while it provided greatly for our family, I know there were downsides like the amount of stress that it put on my parents, the long hours, oh yeah, and THE STRESS! Growing up in a grocery store meant playing in boxes while shelves were being stocked, fighting with my sister about who got to crawl under dad's desk to hunt for loose change that may have been dropped (intentionally) while counting the register drawers, and having a hard time planning vacations due to the unpredictability of the employees or equipment.

The point is, as an adult, I'm not a fan of grocery stores. I like to get in, be efficient, and get out. There's no dilly-dallying to see what's new or different. You'd best get out of my way if you see me charging full speed down the aisles with my list in my heels. The heels are an audible warning for people to move out of my way. Shopping at the grocery store isn't like shopping at a retail store. I don't find it fun or exciting. It's a utilitarian trip that needs to happen for me to keep the people in my house alive.

However, just because I have to go to the grocery store, that doesn't mean that I have to spend all day there. The most efficient way to grocery shop is to earn your black belt in meal planning and food management. I like to eliminate inefficiencies in any process that I have to engage in regularly, and minimizing food waste, making efficient trips to the store, and planning your meals will help you to earn an adulty gold star in meal planning.

Step 1: Make a Master Meal List & Organize Your Recipes

No matter how many people you are cooking for on the regular, you likely have a myriad of dinner recipe options. If you're a collector of recipes like I am, you need to organize them so that they can be found quickly and easily. I use all different colored plastic folders, and on the inside pockets, I have written "Haven't Tried" on the left pocket and "Tried" on the right pocket. On the outside, I write the category: Soups, Breads, Desserts, Chicken, White Meat, Beef, etc.

Once you have organized and cataloged your recipes into folders, you can compile a master meal list of all the options categorized by whatever you named your folders. My master meal list has things broken down by the aforementioned categories, but the items that can be made on a weeknight after school/work are highlighted in green for easier finding.

Top tip: Put that list in a plastic sleeve because it will get gross otherwise.

Step 2: Make the Menu

I have three magnet-backed list notepads on the side of my refrigerator. The first list is the menu, the second is the grocery store list, and the third is the warehouse/club store list. When I prepare to make my menu for the next week, I get the master meal list, the three notepads from the side of the refrigerator, and my calendar.

Shopping at the grocery store happens on Thursdays or Fridays so my menus start on the weekends and end on a Friday (the next trip to the store day). You can't shop for fresh items too soon before use, or they will spoil, turn into slime in the refrigerator, and eventually come to life to kill you in your sleep!

First, I check my calendar to see what my weeknights look like. If I have even less time than normal because of a Parent Teacher Organization meeting, that shorter timeframe means a quicker, easier meal. If my kids are at their dad's house, and it's just me, I don't cook. Are you crazy? I forage for food like a wild animal on those nights.

When my hubby is in town, I make things I know he likes, and on the weekends, I try to make more elaborate dinners that make leftovers that I can send back with him when he heads south to work.

Step 3: Make the Shopping Lists

Once the weekly menu is made, go to your recipe folders, and pull out the recipes for the week. Stack them in order of usage, and then write all the ingredients on the grocery store list and warehouse store list. Once you've written down all the ingredients, place the recipes on the counter where they can be accessed in order. Tear off the disorganized original grocery list, and rewrite the list in the order of the store. Repeat the procedure with the warehouse store list. I promise you that reordering your list will save you so much time!

> *Dick and Jane liked their food on a whim. If Dick was in the mood for pizza, they went out for pizza. If Jane didn't feel like stopping at the grocery store on her way home, she picked the restaurant, and they met there. Even if Jane had planned and*

purchased groceries for a specific dinner, if she didn't feel like cooking, they went out, and the food spoiled. In the mornings when they went their separate ways to work, they each stopped at a gas station for snacks and a drink... and sometimes a donut.

"Dick," Jane said one day, "Do you know how much we are spending on food?"

"No, honey, why?" Dick asked naively.

"Well, you know how we talked about cutting back spending and putting more toward our retirement? Well, I think we are spending way too much going out and on snacks at the gas stations," she explained. "I've been working on our budget, and it just seems really high."

"What do you think that we should do?" asked Dick. I have a box of my grandma's recipes, and I've been meaning to open it and try some, but I just haven't found the motivation. Maybe now is the time," said Jane.

"Oh, do you have that one for her meatloaf? My mouth starts watering every time I think about it." Dick said with childlike excitement.

"I think so. I'll get them out tonight and see if I can organize them into a system. Maybe we can make a plan to try them all with a menu. What do you think?" she asked as she immediately saw the answer on her excited husband's face. "I'll help you cook if you'd like. Or I could go to the store if you want to do the cooking," he offered in his exciement to help make his homemade food dreams a reality.

Laughing, Jane accepted the help, and together they worked toward their own effective meal-planning system. "Dick, I saw those energy drinks at the warehouse store… the ones you like to get at the gas station. They're so much cheaper if we get them in bulk." Jane added.

"Really? How about we take a trip to the store and see what else they have that might make sense to get there too?"

A few months later, Dick and Jane had streamlined their food processes, and they were able to contribute enough each month toward both of their IRAs to be able to maximize their annual contributions.

The great thing about meal planning is that even your food will be efficient. There shouldn't be any food waste if you stick to your menu, you will only have to make one trip to the stores (saving time and gas), and bonus: your family will always know the answer to "What's for dinner?"

HE SAID

She: When you were the primary caregiver for your daughter after your divorce, how did you go about planning meals and making dinners?

He: I would just buy stuff that I knew I could make.

She: Like the day of or the week before?

He: Both. I would just buy the stuff to make meals for two to three days at a time. I didn't mind going back and forth to grocery stores. When you live in a very small town, it's not a huge problem. Plus, my kid only ate certain things.

She: So… how many different meals were in the rotation?

He: I'd make tacos, spaghetti, um…

She: You're such a bachelor.

He: Chicken, um, what else did I make?

She: Hamburger Helper?

He: No. Never Hamburger Helper.

She: *(Giggling)*

He: I don't remember. It's been so long since I've cooked anything.

She: In what ways do you think that people could be more efficient with their resources when it comes to food?

He: Meal planning is good, don't shop when you're hungry and buy a bunch of crap that will expire before you get a chance to eat it.

She: Don't you do that like every week?

He: Pretty much, but I don't buy that much food.

She: You used to go to the store without a list, and then you'd text me later and say you bought a whole pie and that it was gone.

He: Yeah, well that's a meal. Half the pie in the morning for breakfast, and half the pie for supper.

She: That's meal planning?

He: Yeah.

She: Okaaaayyy. Where do you think people waste the most money when it comes to food?

He: Hmm… eating out blows a lot of money.

She: Hmm. That's not what I thought you were going to say.

He: What do you think it would be?

She: I think there's a lot of attrition when it comes to people that don't plan the meals and just buy a bunch of stuff at the store, they didn't plan to use it, and then it goes bad. That's just wasteful. Or people who stop at the gas station when they could buy stuff at the grocery store or warehouse store and save a lot of money that way. So… when you take me out to dinner, it's a complete waste of money?

He: No, but there's people that eat out a lot.

She: Yeah, there are people I work with who seem to eat out a lot but always complain about not having any money. In what ways would you be willing to contribute to the cause in order for there to be more homemade dinners in your future?

He: What do you mean?

She: To negate the amount of eating out.

He: We don't really eat out that much anyway.

She: That's because I know it's expensive. Usually, if I want a night off, I schedule a dinner out.

He: I could make meals, I guess.

She: So, your answer is to step in and take over making meals in order to avoid going out?

He: I would make stuff the way I like to make it, and I'm not going to curtail to please other people.

She: What's that supposed to mean? I don't do that.

He: I won't eat spaghetti without meat in it.

She: Why do you think I don't serve it to you?

He: I like my spaghetti with meat, and I think it's super good, but your kids don't like it that way.

She: Yeah, but I make my sauce from scratch so we wouldn't have you make spaghetti.

He: That's fine.

She: Plus, if you did make dinner, and I told them to eat it, they would have to eat it. That's the rule.

Meal planning can be a very streamlined process, but as with any streamlined process, it will take effort to learn it and implement it on the front end. While it is a bit of work, meal planning can benefit you in other ways. You'll eat out less and save more money by making food at home. Homemade food is also better for you in that you know exactly what is and is NOT going into it.

Buying in bulk and planning ahead will save you money as well by reducing impulse buys at the gas station where everything is overpriced. Now, I would NEVER suggest that you stop dining out. Never. If you and your partner aren't taking turns cooking, you can do what I do, and when it's his turn, I make reservations.

Chapter 11:

I Have a Selfie Stick, and I'm Not Afraid to Use It!

SHE SAID

Have you ever visited a touristy place and seen the gaggle of Asian tourists with the fancy cameras clicking happily away at everything? I'm not trying to stereotype my race because I have witnessed this phenomenon. Even though I'm adopted, I think that photography is bred into our genes as Asians.

Sometimes I even tell people that I was born with a selfie stick in my hands. Why do I make fun of myself and my race? Some people would be ashamed of how many pictures they are seen taking in public, especially selfies with a selfie stick… but I have NO shame when it comes to torturing my friends and family with my array of selfie sticks. Why? Because I'm on the extreme of one end, many people don't take enough photos of their lives and their families. If they do take photos, however, the picture taker is often missing from the images.

My love of photography goes way back to high school when I picked it up as a hobby and shot with 35mm film. That is how old I am... 35mm-film-camera old. I got my first DSLR (Digital Single Lens Reflex or "Big Camera") around when my first son was born. What better excuse to spend thousands of dollars than the birth of your first child, no? Since then, I have taken so many pictures of my family that my children are the most well-trained phototakers ever. Sometimes when I call their names to get their attention, they automatically turn toward me with plastered-on smiles because they assume I'm taking a photo even when I'm not. It's hilarious.

When I am poised to take their photo and only one of them whips around to pose, that child pokes the other and points to me, "Mommy's taking a picture!" Now they coach themselves... I love it! My oldest is a great smiler and has never needed much coaching to look naturally happy, but my youngest has what I call the picture "pooping face". The pooping face is when his mouth is smiling but not his eyes, and he looks uncomfortable and unnatural. I have had to use different tactics to get him to give good picture-worthy smiles: tickling him, making him say funny words, even stooping to potty and farting jokes. Desperate times.

I have even gone so far as to rebuff the school photos and do impromptu photo sessions with my kids every fall in the woods at our house. I prefer to be in control of the potential pooping face, the backdrop, the cleanliness of the outfits, etc. Plus, I take photos of them together, and these are the photos that get sent to the grandparents.

When I met Andy, he told me that he hated getting his picture taken and that he never allowed anyone including friends, family, and significant others to post photos of him on social media. So sorry, husband, but I'm a picture-taking social media-loving person, and I wasn't about to change to be with someone new. From the moment he met me, he became aware that there's no telling me what I can and can't do so he has also become an expert at taking selfies with me. Adapt to survive in my household! It took a LONG time for him to figure out how to smile correctly in photos to negate his version of the pooping face. I remember seeing a photo that we had taken, and asking him, "What were you doing in this picture? Whatever you were doing, you need to replicate that every time we take a selfie because your face actually looks happy!"

"I was laughing at something," he explained. I love that picture, but I hate the mustache that he decided was a good idea to grow at that time.

"It's my Dirk Diggler," he said proudly. "You look like an old porn star," I shot back.

"Yeah, that's why it's cool," he said determined to keep it. It's gone now, by the way, and it hasn't returned.

Did he figure out how to smile better for all subsequent selfies after the mustache picture? You bet he did. He's military, they're hardcore at following orders. Plus, he always says, "If I do a good job from the start, it'll be over faster." He's not wrong. I'll retake and retake photos until I get one I'm satisfied with. "Don't move!" I instruct the family as I run to check the photo up close.

With the invention of convenient cell phone cameras, people have become much better at capturing moments. However, that does not mean that these moments include the picture taker, and these moments aren't necessarily good pictures either.

When my uncle passed away, my parents asked me if I would design the program for his funeral. Of course, I would. I was a graphic designer for two decades, and they paid for my education, and it was family. The program was to have a photo of my uncle from his time in the Merchant Marines and a recent photo. Whom do you think they asked for a more recent photo of him? The picture-taking psycho of the family: me.

I only saw my uncle maybe once a year around the time when he drove north from Mississippi to visit my parents and to attend their high school reunion. The reunion usually fell around the same time as my children's combined birthday party, which was around June 7th, my uncle's birthday, my dad's birthday, and my youngest son's birthday. June is a big month for our family because my oldest was born in June too.

The last time I had seen my uncle before he passed was the year before in June. Of course I called everyone together for a photo; it's my job in the family to do that. I'm happy to do it. The photo I took of him with my dad was the most current, high-quality photo and was the image requested for the funeral program. It was in that moment of designing the program that I realized how important my role as the family photographer is. Every family should have one, and why can't it be you?

That family photo selfie stick session was only one of the hundreds of group photos that I have initiated because I understand the value of capturing moments when people gather. Most people don't want to inconvenience others by making everyone get up, assemble, and stand together for a picture, but if no one does it, those moments are gone. I think I'm the holder of some of the last family pictures with Andy's grandmother because I made everyone stand together and take them. When we make our annual trip to Iowa, I always make sure to try to capture pictures of Andy with his 95-year-old grandfather. Last year, I took videos of him telling stories because I want to make sure that some memories are preserved.

When I worked in long-term senior care, I oversaw gathering the obituary information for residents who had passed for the monthly memorial ceremony. There were so many instances where you could tell no one in the family had taken a recent photo of their loved one in quite some time, and I found that to be such a tragedy.

And it's not only the elderly that can pass without being memorialized in photos. Anyone can also go at any time... you see these photos on the news. Whenever I see a bad photo on the news of someone who passed suddenly, I always wonder why someone didn't have a better photo. Today with easy camera access, there are no excuses not to suck less at taking group photos.

> *Jane's friend Sandy had invited her out to dinner with a bunch of friends. Upon arrival, Sandy called everyone together to take a group selfie. "Sandy, people are staring at us," Jane whispered as her cheeks flushed with embarrassment. "Oh, who cares!" replied Sandy, immune to public embarrassment.*

> *"Okay, everyone get closer. If you can't see your face in the phone, you aren't in the picture," she instructed. People were indeed starting to stare, but Jane did as she was told and squeezed into the photo. "Everyone smile!" instructed Sandy.*

> *When the dinner was over, and everyone was heading to their cars, Jane asked Sandy, "Do you really think that was necessary? It was so embarrassing."*

"Jane, loosen up! I think this might be one of the last times I see my friend Mia. Her husband is waiting for his military deployment assignment, and I wanted to make sure that I captured this moment so that I can print it and give it to her if she ends up leaving." Sandy explained with sadness.

"Well, I guess that's a good reason. I didn't know that she might be leaving. That's sad." Jane said as her embarrassment disappeared.

"I'm glad that you made us do it even if she doesn't end up moving away. We had such a great time. Would you send me a copy of that photo later?" Jane asked. "Of course I will, sweetie," she replied as it started to rain. "Ooh—I'm not waterproof. I'll see you at work on Monday!" Yelled Sandy as she raced off to her car with her handbag over her head.

On Monday morning in the office, Sandy told Jane that Mia found out she'd be moving away. They went to the store at lunch and picked out a sparkly frame that matched Mia's shiny personality. "Sandy, where did you get that selfie stick? I think

> *that maybe I should get one to capture more memories." "Girl, you know where I got it. Where I get everything... on Amazon," she said as they giggled.*

Sometimes I need to remind myself to take photos of my parents when I see them, and it's not a holiday. Why? That's a good question. I just realized that I'm sucking in this area. I think the reason that I don't is that in my mind, my parents aren't supposed to die. They are my parents and should always be there because I need them to be there. I don't want to think of their NOT being there. Regardless, I'm going to suck less at making sure to take more pictures of them too.

Everyone who knows me knows that if you've got plans with me, there's a 95% chance you will be photographed. I make sure to get into photos too; that's why I have the selfie stick. Many moms don't seem to want to get in front of the camera. Some of the reasons are that they think they gained weight, they didn't have time to do their hair or makeup, they aren't wearing cute clothes, or that someone has to take the picture. Excuses,

excuses, excuses. What if something happened to Mom, and there were no photos of her with her family? I don't think the family would care about any of her reasons not to be in the photos so BE IN THE PHOTOS.

No one will look at those photos of you and judge you as harshly as you judge yourself. They will look and see a loving mom, a great sister, a fun friend, and a wonderful spouse. Get a selfie stick, get the family together, and capture those memories! If you're embarrassed to do it in public, blame me, "My super weird friend told me to take this picture and send it to her!" You're welcome.

HE SAID

She: Why don't you like getting your picture taken?

He: Cuz it's annoying.

She: That's the only reason?

He: I don't know what the purpose is. I feel like it's to show off to people, and I don't find that cool.

She: Hmm. Why do you let me do it?

He: Because I love you, and I'll let you do just about anything you want.

She: Are there people that you wish you had more photos of?

He: Mmmmm... not really.

She: Your dad?

He: I have photos of my dad.

She: You don't wish you had more of them?

He: Not really.

She: Are there people that you think you should get or have more photos of now?

He: I don't have any photos of my daughter and me from the last few years. I don't know. I wish I had taken more photos when I was in the military, but I don't regret things.

She: I'm talking about in the context of the fact that my parents asked me to make the memorial program for my uncle's funeral and how hard it is to find pictures of people when no one takes pictures. If I died, and there were no photos of me, you wouldn't be upset about that?

He: *(Laughing)* I have in my phone right now, I guarantee you at least 100 photos of you.

She: *(Laughing)* That's not what I'm saying though. If it wasn't that way. I know I'm extreme, but if I was in the opposite extreme and never wanted to have my picture taken, and then I just died….

He: Well then it would be different then.

She: Don't you see a value there?

He: There's more to you in memories, I don't need pictures. 1,000 pictures don't make it any more real than one picture.

She: UGH!

He: You can't project your value system onto me. That makes no sense.

She: Well then you'll love this last question, and stop being a sh*thead.

He: I'm not being a sh*thead.

She: We are almost done.

He: I'm just saying.

She: Stop it.

He: You're projecting things onto a man that…

She: You suck at this then. Just answer the last question; I'm tired. Do you think that selfie sticks are something people should invest in, why or why not?

He: *(With a slightly provocating tone)* If you want to take pictures, a selfie stick definitely makes it easier.

She: I swear to God, I'm gonna smack you right now.

He: It definitely makes it easier than having to hold your phone out, and you get better photographs, so yes, if you want quality photographs, then you probably want a selfie stick.

She: Are you pandering right now?

He: Yes, it makes sense. It works easier and logistically makes sense.

She: I feel like you are lying down on the railroad tracks right now.

(Both laughing through the conversation)

He: It's easier to take a picture with a selfie stick, than not!

She: Oh my God.

He: They wouldn't make them if it wasn't easier to use them. Duh!

I love him so much, but sometimes... UGH! It's a good thing he's not my target demographic for these books.

Capturing the memories of moments with your loved ones is something that we all should aspire to be great at. There's no excuse with the convenience and quality of cell phone camera technology. Even if you hate getting your picture taken, you think you don't look great at the moment, or you don't have a selfie stick, set the timer, and take the picture. Being able to return to those memories is the gift of time travel itself and the only way that you can save that memory for the future.

Don't make excuses for why you don't want to take or be in more photos. If you're reading this chapter, there's time to make a change. Buy a selfie stick, and embarrass yourself and your family when you pose in front of it because no one will look back at that time and remember being embarrassed. They will look back with fondness at the time shared, the love of family, and the moments captured. Oh, and try not to look like you're pooping… unless you are.

Chapter 12:

No More I Love You's

SHE SAID

Some people grew up in households where "I Love You" was said so often that it became second nature. However, some people grow up in households where the sentiment is silently understood. My childhood leaned more toward the quiet understanding of love. Don't get me wrong, my parents were always showing me that they loved me, but they didn't say it much. As I got older, they started saying it, and truth be told, I had a hard time saying it back. Why? Not because I didn't love them but because it just seemed awkward.

When birthdays or other card-giving holidays came around, I would scour the card rack for the funniest cards and avoid the mushy "I love you" cards, usually as I muttered an audible "Ick" sound while talking to myself. Sometimes we use laughter as an avoidance tactic when it comes to dealing with feelings, and that's what I must have been doing. While the avoidance of mushy cards led to several hilarious years of exchanging cards with the reoccurring image of a sloppy guy wearing booty jean shorts overlaid on different card backgrounds, I was sucking at I Love You's.

Earlier this year, my dad suffered some broken ribs and a crack around his knee replacement when he fell at home. He had to be taken by ambulance to a trauma hospital two hours away. While he was in the hospital, I realized that my parents weren't going to live forever, and the reality of their immortality hit me. I sent a voice message to my mom's phone for her to play for him since he didn't have his cell phone with him. In that message, I made sure to say that I loved him, and I felt bad for the times I hadn't said it.

Not long after that incident, while my dad was still recovering from his injuries, that's when his brother passed away. As my parents were making the three-day trip south to where his brother resided, they called me to check-in. At the end of the call, I heard myself say, "I love you guys", and it wasn't awkward. What had changed? The reality of their mortality and I suppose some growth in maturity on my end.

Saying "I love you" is so simple but can also be so complicated. I don't have any issue saying it freely to my husband or my kids... or my cat. Why was it so hard to say it to my parents? Why did I suck at I love yous? Thank goodness that with life experience comes wisdom, and with wisdom comes changes for the better. I think that if we are fortunate enough to realize what and who we have before it's too late, we can make sure to let our loved ones know that we love them by never missing an opportunity to say it.

> *Jane loved her husband so much, but there were days or even weeks when he just got on her every nerve. She was starting to wonder if it was she who was changing or if he was doing more things to annoy her. While Jane loved a house where everything was in its place and void of clutter, Dick seemed to be cluttering up the spaces that she*

specifically had told him that she didn't want his tools and toys. The thing that was bothering her to the point of madness was his new obsession with rebuilding old radios and the accompanying cords and clutter that came with it. The visual disorganization on a desk in her bedroom was infuriating to her.

"Dick, I thought that we finished the basement and set up that area for you down there so that you could put all of your crap down there instead of on my nice furniture upstairs which, by the way, you have ruined!" Jane screeched with frustration.

"Hello to you too, honey," Dick said as he cautiously entered the house after work.

An uncomfortable silence grew between them as he was exiled to the couch, and she was still too mad to talk to him about anything other than his shortcomings. After a few weeks of only communicating with the bare minimum, the tension between them was growing stronger.

"Oh. My. Gosh, Sandy!" huffed Jane as she barged into Sandy's office on Monday morning. "Dick is *so annoying. He just doesn't listen no matter how many times I tell him to put his crap in the basement! I can't stand to look at those cords and the clutter."*

"Jane, you love Dick. You guys hardly ever fight, and if you do, you kiss and makeup in like an hour," Sandy said as she mocked how lovey their marriage was. "Remember when Dick got in that accident when he was drunk driving and how worried you were about the thought of losing him?" Sandy said with sincere concern. "Think about how you would have felt if something happened to Dick while you two were in this silly fight."

After a few moments of quiet consideration, Jane muttered, "You're right, Sandy. I am blowing this fight way out of proportion. I think maybe it's this new project at work with the tight deadline that's making me crazy and causing me to be ruder to him than I normally would be." As she thought through the real reason behind the juvenile way she was treating her husband, she started to feel bad... really bad.

"Thanks, lady, I appreciate you so much," Jane acknowledged as she got up to get some fresh air. The more she thought about how much she was sucking at being a good partner, the more she was motivated to make up for her petulant behavior. She left work a little early and stopped at the store to buy him some old-timey décor for the wall behind the desk in their bedroom.

When Dick came home that afternoon, Jane immediately rushed to apologize for her behavior and lead him upstairs to show him what she had done. "Wow, Jane, that's really cool! I thought you hated this radio project and wanted it out of the bedroom. I'm confused." he said. "I just want you to be happy," she began. "I was stressed out at work, and it came out as freaking out at you about something silly. I'm sorry. It's your house too, and I love you so much. I want you to be happy."

"I love you too, Jane. Thank you for apologizing, and I'll try harder to keep my other hobbies and clutter in the basement." Dick compromised as they made up... twice, in the same room that had been the location of the fighting in the first place.

Just this morning as I left the house to run an errand, I saw that my husband hadn't put the trash bin out at the end of the driveway as I had requested the night before. Without thinking about how I should approach him and without remembering that he never does anything intentionally to piss me off, I called him from the car.

> **Me:** Why didn't you put out the trash bin like I asked you last night?
>
> **Hubby:** You never told me to do that.
>
> **Me:** Yes, I did! I specifically told you that the trash needed to go out to the end of the driveway.
>
> **Hubby:** No, you didn't.
>
> **Me:** I always know when trash day is. What if we miss it!? Can you do it right now?!

Was that the end of it? Was I done being crazy? No. I texted him on the way home and said that I would be there in five minutes and asked if he could help unload the groceries. Still upset from the trash conversation, I barged into the house with the first load and exploded at him for not being at the door ready to help.

After he calmly got up and helped without snapping back at me, I realized that I was melting down at him for no reason. While I know for a fact that I asked for the trash bin to be put out the night before, my reaction wasn't what it should have been, and I immediately apologized. He's so much more emotionally mature than I am, and his calm reactions to my freakouts usually result in my realizing and vocalizing more that I love him.

While it's easy for me to make sure that say "I love you" to him when he's on a long drive to see me, it's not always as easy to remember that no matter the circumstance, the call, the fight about something dumb… "I love you" should always be the last thing we say to the people we cherish the most. Always.

HE SAID

She: Have you always been one to say "I Love You" freely to the people you love?

He: Yeah, oh yeah. Absolutely.

She: Is there anyone you wish you'd have said "I love you" more to?

He: No.

She: Do you think that you and I would ever be in a scenario where you wouldn't end a conversation with "I love you", like a fight or something?

He: No.

She: Why?

He: I don't do that. I don't play those games.

She: You couldn't get that upset?

He: Oh, I get that upset, but I don't with you. What's the point? At this age (53), death is around every corner. You can't be doing that kind of stuff.

She: Have you ever been in a relationship where you avoided saying "I love you"?

He: Yeah, I suppose.

She: You don't know?

He: I think that's pretty common.

She: So, the answer is yes?

He: Yeah.

She: Don't be so vague. Has it always been easy for you to say "I love you" to your parents?

He: Yeah.

My other half sees life very clearly whereas sometimes I struggle to. Maybe the reason is that he's lived a decade more than I have, and he has had those years to mature and have his worldview shaped by experiences. Or, maybe he's just amazing, which is probably the reason I married him. Regardless of how he came by his wisdom, I'm always thankful to have someone that is grounded reminding me how simple the important things can be.

You don't always have to like your family or your partner, but you always have to love them. For the most part, the people we love and who love us back are not trying to irritate us for fun. Most often when issues arise, the reason they get blown out of proportion is factors and stressors outside of the actual issue either from work, kids, other family, or a deeper issue in the relationship.

The only things that are guaranteed in life are death and taxes as I was reminded of at the double family funeral I attended last week. If you find yourself lucky to be enlightened about the fact that you should cherish your family while they are with you, you have given yourself a gift that no one should take for granted. No matter the reason for the call, the visit, or the text, remember that your family should be loved unconditionally… and don't leave any "I Love You's" left unsaid.

Chapter 13:

Don't Be a Lemming, Be a Leader

SHE SAID

Lemmings are cute little guinea pig-like rodents that people reference when making comments about following others into stupid or dangerous situations. While adorable, they're not known for their leadership qualities. They are blind followers, and blind followers don't defy mediocrity and rise above.

Being a leader isn't easy unless you come by it naturally, and yes, there is a place for leaders and a place for followers. It wouldn't work if everyone was a leader, or a follower, for that matter. I wasn't always a leader. Back in school, you wouldn't have even known I existed, I was so quiet. However, through different experiences and adversities in my life, I have come to embrace leadership and the challenges and responsibilities that come along with it.

> Dick had been at his job for quite a few years through several supervisor changes. While he liked the company and what it stood for, he also felt like he was being overlooked and was becoming just a number to the higher-ups. "I feel like I'm a bit bored with my job," Dick confessed to his friend Bob whose office was one door away from Dick's.
>
> "Have you applied for a better job or asked for a promotion?" asked Bob. "It sure seems like there's enough turnover at the next level up for you to catch one of the openings," he continued. "Yeah, I did, but after getting turned down, I wasn't sure if I would look stupid if I tried again," Dick explained.
>
> "Aren't they always looking for more people to be on that community outreach committee that decides where we all go for a day to help out?" Bob asked as he threw a tiny basketball into a similarly tiny hoop on the back of his office door.

"Oh yeah, maybe that's a good place to start." Dick agreed as he picked up the ball and tossed it playfully at his friend's head.

Over the next few months, Dick tried to speak up more in meetings, and he joined the community outreach group at work. When the head of the group got a job in another state, Dick found himself being nominated for the position, which he gladly accepted. Six months later, Dick was approached by his boss about a supervisory promotion. "Dick, I've noticed you really stepping up your game here at work, and I think you should apply for this new role that oversees a team of five." *His boss suggested.*

"Thank you! I sure will," he responded.

Shortly after that conversation, Dick found himself in the role he had been working toward, and he took Bob out to celebrate. "I knew you could do it," *Bob said as they shared a beer.* "You just needed to find your own way there, boss!"

> *"Thanks for the encouragement. I'll try not to be too hard on you," joked Dick as they celebrated together.*

In my current job, attending community events and presentations is one of the aspects that I love because I get to be out making connections. At the end of one lunch event where the speaker was talking about bringing more diversity to Duluth, I happened to raise my hand when she asked if anyone had any questions. I'm always that person with a million questions, but I'm not always quick to raise my hand in a room full of community and business leaders unless I have a good reason.

Since diversity and race are my hot-button issues, and I found the presentation to be lacking in solution and message, I may have aggressively interrogated the speaker about the details of her plans to bring more diversity to the area. I mean, I was also so angry that I sort of blacked out a little, but boy was my blood boiling that day.

Not thinking much about my public interlude, I moved on as my life grew busier with my impending wedding. Several months after I had arrived back home from my honeymoon, I was checking my emails, and I had a message inviting me to write an article about leadership for a local print publication associated with the organizers of that lunch meeting. Odd. Why me? I asked myself as I perused through old issues to see who had contributed to this section before. I wasn't a business leader, and I didn't have flashy titles like the ones I was seeing listed.

"Can I ask how I was chosen to contribute to this publication?" I asked because why wouldn't I? "Sometimes we ask the people who raise their hands at our events to contribute to this section about leadership. Ah ha! That made sense. Anyone bold enough to raise their hand in a room full of hundreds of people in formal business attire at the swankiest ballroom in town had to have some thoughts about leadership.

I almost said no, but I know myself, and that's my first reaction to anything that scares me even a little bit. After letting the thought simmer for a while, I decided that it was an honor to be asked and an opportunity that I would be stupid to pass up. While on the cool-down walk uphill during one of my before-dawn runs, I drafted the article below for submission.

> Leadership wears many faces *(and many show-stopping pairs of stilettos, in my case)*. Some leaders are born, some are formed through adverse circumstances, and some are taught. Leadership, much like parenting, requires leading by example and always striving for the highest level of success in all aspects of life:
>
> - in how you treat others with empathy,
> - in how you carry yourself,
> - in the words that you choose,
> - in your attitude, dedication, and consistency,
> - in your ability to think quickly, confidently, and decisively,
> - and in how you can always be trusted to get the job done.

Management and leadership are <u>not</u> interchangeable. Leadership cannot be defined by a title or by how many people one supervises. Some managers are not good leaders, and some people who are not managers are great leaders. **So, what is the recipe for a great leader?**

A great leader has a positive attitude and is willing to do anything to succeed, whether that means taking out the trash or running a board meeting. Being empathetic but not a pushover, being respected but not feared, and being able to command a room without uttering one word are characteristics that also define a great leader. Just as animals can instinctually sense who will back down from a fight and who will be strong enough to defend the herd, a great leader has a palpable confidence that others can sense and will inadvertently follow.

Leading by example builds trust, and trust earns respect. This pathway to great leadership works for everyone from veteran staff to one's own children. When you hold yourself to the same high standards that you expect of your subordinates *(essentially the opposite of* "do as I say, not as I do"*)*, you will be successful.

Great leaders are teachers, but more importantly, they need to be teachable, especially by their subordinates. Having the ability to listen while meeting others where they are but also helping them to reach their potential, and having the ability to be an in- and out-of-the-box problem solver are also the markings of a great leader.

Much like palm trees, great leaders may bend to the ground in storms but will right themselves and stand tall when the storm clears; and while great leaders may not wear a cape or be superheroes like Spiderman, they are always highly aspirational with a character shrouded in humility.

(Duluthian, November-December 2022)

In my current job, I don't have direct reports, but I do lead volunteer organizations. However, as I stated in the article, leadership is often a mindset and a willingness to step up and take charge in situations where there may be chaos and no clear leader. Leadership does have its downsides like when something bad happens, and the responsibility falls fully onto the leader, but good leaders position themselves to handle any situation with professionalism, integrity, and dignity. It is because of these qualities that others often see them as aspirational and people after whom they will follow… just not off a cliff with the other cute lemmings.

HE SAID

She: Would you say that you are a leader or a follower?

He: Both.

She: Okay. Moreso one or the other, in general?

He: I don't know.

She: What do you mean, you don't know?

He: I don't have to lead.

She: That's not what I asked you. So, if there was a scenario where you could be either, would you prefer one or the other?

He: I like not having responsibility. I like having responsibility for myself, so, I guess a better follower.

She: Hmm. In what circumstances have you been a leader?

He: I've been a trainer before, I'm a senior officer... my leading style is to lead by example.

She: I didn't ask you about your leadership style. What about in the Army?

He: Yeah, there too. I'm a Ranger. Rangers lead the way.

She: What qualities do you possess that make you a good leader?

He: I'm dependable, have integrity, and am very rational.

She: Have you ever felt like you've failed in a leadership role, and why?

He: Yeah, because I could have done a better job and handled things better.

She: What are we talking about, specifically?

He: At work, at home...

She: Here?!

He: Yeah, I guess I could take more of a leadership role here.

She: Is that what you were talking about when you said "home"?

He: I'm talking about home... home... I guess I could take more of a leadership role here.

She: Can you concentrate, please?!

He: I'm concentrating.

She: What do you think makes a great leader?

He: Somebody who knows how to follow.

She: What?!

He: Someone who knows how to follow will know how to take information from those who are subordinates.

She: A follower makes a great leader?

He: Yeah, you can't be a great leader if you don't know how to follow.

She: *(Mumbling)* Okay, these are weird answers.

He: Well, do you disagree?

She: No, I kind of expected something a little deeper than that. So, what makes a bad leader?

He: Somebody who isn't willing to take responsibility for the failures of the people beneath them, or someone who thinks they're always right and leads from an egotistical point of view.

She: Do you think that if someone wants to be a good leader, that there are ways to do that if you aren't a natural leader?

He: No, I don't think so.

She: Why?

He: Because there are parts of your character that you can't change. People always have a certain response, like when things are stressful, they might do something underhanded if that comes naturally to them. Those people, you can't change.

She: There's no other circumstance if someone aspired to be a leader that they could be a good leader?

He: They could be a *better* leader. If you can set a good example, and maintain it while having good ethical characteristics, sometimes those things are enough to inspire people to follow you. You can't be a good leader if people don't believe in you. You can't fake that.

She: But what if someone wants to get a leadership role in their job?

He: Just because you have a job that says you're a leader doesn't mean you're a good leader and are effective at it.

Even though my husband and I didn't come to the same conclusion by following the same path, we did come to the same conclusion that a job title does not always equate to good leadership.

Leadership plays an important role in life and society. We look to our leaders to know how to act, what to believe, and what we should aspire to be. Bad leadership can be a detriment to an organization, a company, or even a group of friends, but great leadership can encourage others to achieve goals, be better people, and bring success to others.

If you feel as though you have the strength of character and the fortitude to withstand storms that may hit without warning, then leadership is something you should work your way toward. Even if you don't supervise in your job, there are other great ways to be a leader or work your way into leadership: volunteer on a board of directors, chair a committee at work, express your ideas, and don't be afraid to speak your mind. Speaking your mind pushes you to have to defend your perspective, and that confidence is something that others will follow. Once you embrace your leadership abilities, you may find yourself presented with opportunities that you never dreamed possible.

Chapter 14:

It's Not Failure If You Learn from It

SHE SAID

Stepping out of our comfort zones and taking chances are things that scare the average person, but what would happen if we got out of our heads and embraced every opportunity that life presented? What's the worst that could happen? We could make an ass out of ourselves, we could fail, or we could lose resources. Yes, these scenarios are scary because the outcomes are unknown, but isn't the scenario of living life with regrets also scary?

My husband had a buddy in the army who always said, "I'd rather regret doing something than regret not doing something." That's the mindset of living life to the fullest, grabbing the bull by the horns, or not making opportunity knock twice, or whatever adage you prefer to make the point relatable.

There are many opportunities, like the invitation I received to write an article about leadership, that may only come once in your lifetime. Would I have regretted not pushing myself and saying yes to that opportunity? For sure! Sometimes windows will open for us, and other times we will need to find windows to run toward, but regardless of how we come to opportunities in life, we should be embracing the chance to learn something new.

There have been many skills that I have found the opportunity to learn like during the COVID-19 pandemic that shut down the salons. In case it's not painfully evident at this point, I'm super high-maintenance. I had been a regular customer every three weeks at the nail salon, and when I couldn't go, I panicked. Because I was friends on social media with one of the co-owners of the salon (note the side benefit of making friends with EVERYONE everywhere), I asked what I would need to replicate the acrylic nail gel polish procedure at home.

The first time I did my own nails was a hot disaster, but hey, I was the only person with nails that had even been attempted to be done recently. As the pandemic dragged on, I figured out my own system to achieve the results I was used to, and over four years later, I'm still doing them myself from the comfort of my kitchen. Had I not found that window of opportunity to run toward, I never would have learned a new skill that has saved me thousands of dollars.

The pandemic and not being able to do anything outside the house also forced me to try to find a new hobby for my Type A+ personality. I got it in my head that I wanted to do a podcast about relationships with my husband, who responded, "I never agreed to that."

"Oh, yes you did. Remember that trip to Iowa when we were listening to that dating podcast, and you said, 'We could do so much better than this'?" I asked.

"I don't remember that," he responded.

"I have notes. We're doing it." This was my parting sentiment before I started to research and buy equipment.

I'm one of those weird people who loves a challenge. I get obsessed with figuring it out, then I get obsessed about being great at it, and after I feel like I've mastered it, then I get bored and do something else. That cycle seems to run for about a year. Why that is, I have no idea. I'm just consistent in my weirdness, I guess. Regardless, my quest for learning and growing drives me to seek out new opportunities.

> When Jane was in high school, she was in choir and the show choir. She loved to sing, and she was great at it, winning awards for solo performances and even singing the national anthem for a high school basketball game. As she got older, she continued to sing in the college choir and in some elective singing classes.
>
> A year after she graduated from college, she had a serious boyfriend who turned to her in the car one

afternoon and said, "Would you please stop singing along to the radio? It's annoying."

"Oh, I didn't realize that. I'll stop," she said as all those years of confidence building seeped out of her, and she found herself only able to sing when she was alone in the shower or car.

"I didn't know you were a singer," said Sandy one day in the office when they were talking about the latest episode of a reality singing show.

"Yeah, I used to love it, and I think I was pretty good," she said with sadness.

"Why did you stop?" Sandy pushed. As she recanted the story, Sandy got angry. "Well, that's bullsh*t! How rude!" she exclaimed, ready to find that boy and serve him with a proper b*tch slap.

"I just can't get that confidence back. Dick hasn't even heard me sing," she confessed.

"What's stopping you from getting back into it now?" asked Sandy.

"I don't know. I have no confidence in myself anymore when it comes to singing. What if he was right, and I suck at it?" she asked.

"I'm sure that isn't the case. You won gold medals!" Sandy urged.

That weekend when the pair had planned a double date, Jane asked, "Where are we going?" when Sandy and Alan arrived to pick them up. "It's a surprise," Sandy said with a giddy clap. "Well, I really don't care because I'm starving," Jane responded not giving it a second thought.

As they pulled up to an unfamiliar place, Jane's face turned pale. "A karaoke bar? I'm not going in there." Said Jane defiantly as she re-fastened her seat belt and crossed her arms. "You don't sing," Dick said to his wife, "So why are you so adamant about not going inside? It could be fun to watch."

Narrowed eyes of anger daggered into Sandy as she yanked Jane out of the car and into the bar. "I'll buy you a drink, and maybe you'll change your mind," chirped Sandy, unphased by the death stare her friend was giving her.

"I'll eat, but I'm not singing," mumbled Jane.

A few drinks in, Jane heard her name being called over the speakers. "We have a special guest tonight who needs a little bit of encouragement... Jane! Come on up here!" said the DJ as the spotlight shined Jane in the eyes. "You're coming with me you witch!" snapped Jane as she grabbed Sandy's hand and forced her on stage with her.

Knowing her friend well enough and that her favorite movie growing up was Disney's Aladdin, the song "A Whole New World" started playing. "I love this song," Jane whispered as her tone softened with her friend. Jane got to sing as Jasmine, and Sandy was her Aladdin. At the end of the song, their husbands and the crowd cheered, and Jane felt like she had gotten some of her confidence back.

"Thank you for pushing me to do that, Sandy" Jane confessed in the car on the way back.

"I forgot how much I used to love singing and how much I missed it," she mused.

> *"Girl, you knew I would push you out of your comfort zone eventually, so I thought I'd just get it out of the way now,"* she jested as they laughed.
>
> *"I almost murdered you,"* Jane said through a smile.
>
> *"I know."*

The more we push ourselves, the more we become comfortable taking on chances, brushing off failures, and continuing to become greater in our strengths. Sometimes life throws us some untimely and very stressful challenges. A few years back, I found myself served with court papers, but I also found myself without the resources to hire an attorney to go toe-to-toe with the opposing attorney. While the details of the situation are irrelevant, that opportunity to learn was one I would have preferred not to have been presented with. Ever.

I panicked. I didn't want to lose, but what could I do? I had no idea how the legal system worked. I went to college for interior design, remember?! Right around that time, I was meeting with a board member for work, and he happened to be an attorney. It was a meet-and-greet lunch that had been planned before the letter from the courts had arrived, so I thought I'd embrace the serendipity. "Do you mind if I ask just one legal question?" I started, unsure of how to navigate the situation without overstepping my boundaries.

"Sure, go ahead!" He offered with his usually jovial demeanor. I laid out the circumstances, and I asked him, "If you could give me one piece of advice, what would it be?" Because he's a great person and one of the most un-lawyery lawyers I know, he started listing off a whole bunch of things that I could do to help myself out. "Write this down…" he instructed with excitement while tearing off a sheet of paper and handing it across the table. Clearly, he was made for his job because he loved it.

After that meeting, I felt like maybe I had a chance of doing it on my own. Maybe. Since I hadn't initiated the legal process, I would receive documents that I needed to respond to. In receiving the documents from an attorney, I was able to mimic the format, layout, and verbiage to create my rebuttals and upload my own supporting documentation to the court's website.

Sure, I doubted whether I was doing the correct thing, and I had several calls with the court to make sure I was filing the right things in the right places, but after the virtual hearing (still in the social distancing of the COVID-19 pandemic) and representing myself on the screen, I was left unsure of how it would end. On Christmas Eve, I was plagued by the knowledge that the verdict was coming in the mail because I had signed up to get the post office's daily mail emails. That was a LONG day.

As I tore into the envelope with fingers that didn't seem to be listening to what I wanted them to do, I scanned the document, trying to find the verdict. No way. I had won! Without a lawyer! And that, my friends, is why I challenge you to push yourself to use any and all opportunities to learn and grow. Never in a billion years would I have assumed that I could have won against a very well-respected lawyer. Never.

Many people who embrace mediocrity used the pandemic as an excuse to let themselves go, complain about things they couldn't change, and stay stagnant in their lives and skill sets. It's the people who want to defy mediocrity and live life without regrets that took that opportunity to be productive, learn something new, and find something positive in a situation that was scary and bizarre.

HE SAID

She: What was the last opportunity that presented itself to you that you turned down?

He: What do you mean?

She: This chapter is about opportunities and pushing yourself.

He: *(Silence)*

She: Didn't they want you to be on the SWAT team?

He: A long time ago.

She: What was the last scenario like that where you decided against it?

He: They've asked me to be a field training officer, and I said no.

She: When did they do that?

He: When I first went back to the street.

She: That was a long time ago.

He: That's the most recent thing I can think of. They pretty much know not to ask me anything now because I'll say no.

She: Okay. What are some opportunities in life that at first scared you, but you rose to the challenge?

He: Probably being a dad.

She: Really!?

He: I thought that was pretty scary.

She: Huh. I thought you were going to say something about the military.

He: That didn't scare me that bad.

She: There's nothing else that scared the crap out of you, but you pushed yourself to do it?

He: No.

She: Hmm. What was the outcome of the challenge of being a parent?

He: She didn't turn out to be a drug addict or pregnant. Those were my big fears, and neither of those things happened.

She: Those were your two fears?

He: As a father of a girl, yes.

She: Okay. Is there anything that you look back at and wish you had done?

He: I wish I would have married someone that was a better fit for me early on so I could have been more successful in life (I'm his second wife, by the way, whom he married later in life), and I wish I would have continued with the aspirations that I had when I was younger.

She: To what end?

He: I wanted to be a helicopter pilot.

She: Really?! I never heard this. I thought you wanted to be D.E.A. or something or special forces or whatever that was.

He: Yeah, but one time I considered trying to get my pilot's license.

She: The way you drive, that'd be horrible.

He: Yeah, probably better off I didn't.

She: Do you feel like you run toward opportunities or challenges that scare you, or do you run away?

He: I don't think either. Any time you make a different life change, it's scary, like when I moved from Iowa to Minnesota. I hate moving.

She: *(Laughing)* Ha! There it is. What scares you, and would you turn it down, and why? Oh, you can't turn it down because you have to move here.

In my lifetime, I have taught myself how to cut my boys' hair, do my own acrylic nails, be a graphic artist, cook, bake, start a charity, write books, create a podcast, manage money, plan for retirement, mount a flat-screen TV to the wall, and so many more things that have pushed me to be better. I used to be that person who was afraid of her shadow, and now, I invite that shadow to come with me as I pursue new opportunities and challenges. Come on, shadow, we got this!

When you find yourself faced with challenges, they should be seen as opportunities, and there are two ways you can go. Runaway scared or stand up and fight. Turn every "I can't" into an "I will", and take ownership of the things you do and how you do them. If you fail, figure out what you can learn from it, and don't make that same mistake again.

Remember, it isn't failure if you learn from it.

Chapter 15:

Be a Good Human

SHE SAID

There aren't just two kinds of people in this world: good people, and sh*tty people. Most people fall into the middle somewhere as they try their best to go about not screwing up their lives or the lives of others. But what can be done to become more of a good human, a person who steps up and contributes extra to society?

If you open your eyes to the world beyond your circle, you will find that many opportunities present themselves to do good in your community. Many non-profits are begging for volunteers, mentors, or board members. Volunteering at these organizations in any capacity is a great way to give back and be an asset to your community.

I haven't always been the community altruist that I am today, but before I started volunteering, I always felt the calling to want to give back, but I just hadn't settled on a place to do so. This is my sixth and final year volunteering as the Parent Teacher Organization President, and I will be stepping away from one role to lead another kid-centric non-profit as the President. While I am passionate about giving back, sometimes my kids hear me grumble as I leave the house past my awake time. As I walked out the door the other night at 5:45 pm on my way to the PTO meeting, I called out to them, "Even though I complain about it sometimes, I still expect you to volunteer when you get older! K bye, love you, don't burn the house down or kill each other."

Being a good human doesn't always have to translate to volunteering. Sometimes you needn't look further than your friend circle or workplace to find a way to be a good human. At work, you may excel at a skill set that you could offer to teach a coworker, or you may have a friend in your social circle who looks up to you that you could encourage and mentor.

Beyond volunteering or mentoring, another way to be a good human is to be optimistic. Positiveness is rare, and people are drawn to it. I'm not advising you to be annoyingly sweet and optimistic to where people want to slap the grin off your face, but you can be a light in many areas to others when it's needed.

> *One Sunday morning as Dick, Jane, and Joy found themselves at church service, a speaker had come to replace the sermon with a presentation about an organization that helps children in need around the world. As they sat down for their usual after-church lunch at the local family restaurant, Joy seemed quieter than usual.*
>
> *"What's the matter, Joy?" Asked Dick with concern.*
>
> *"Nothing. I just feel like maybe I'd like to be part of that program that they were talking about at church. Maybe I could sponsor someone. I think I make enough to afford $28 a month," she said as she ran the numbers in her head.*

"I think that's very adult of you, Joy, and I'm proud of you," said Jane with a smile.

When they arrived home, Joy signed up for the program online, and a week later, she had the information of a young boy in Indonesia. "Mom, I have no idea what to write to him. I don't have a little brother, and I haven't babysat. Can you help me?" she asked Jane.

"Of course. We should also send some pictures, so he knows who he's talking to," she noted as they sat down together.

Each correspondence took about a month because of the international mail and the translating that needed to happen in the middle, but Joy looked forward to getting those letters and always wrote back immediately. She continued to sponsor that little boy through college and also through pricing increases in the program until he finally aged out.

He had decided to become a pastor, he married, and he was ever so thankful for the help that he had gotten from his "Auntie Joy". From the years of sponsorship, Joy was reminded of how lucky she was and that she should always be looking for ways to help others and be a good human.

Joy and I have a lot in common, as I too sponsored a little boy from Indonesia for many, many years. I remember seeing his photo for the first time and not having any idea what to write. 'Why didn't they give me a girl? That would have been so much easier.' I thought, but I was committed to the cause, and I felt a very strong calling to the program. He and I are friends on social media now, and I am thankful for the chance to have helped someone so far away.

Being a good human doesn't have to take a lot of time or money. Sometimes all it takes is being a shoulder to cry on, a friend who listens, or $28 a month. NO, I don't work for that company, and I'm sure it's more than $28 a month now, but a little bit of selflessness and humility will go a long way to helping you become a light in your community and being a good human.

HE SAID

She: What do you think it means to be a good human?

He: Be empathetic, and unselfish, and provide time for people which aren't easy to do. Doing it willingly and happily without feeling obligated.

She: Have you ever volunteered for an organization?

He: Mmmm... I can't remember. I don't think so.

She: Ever? Never?

He: I don't remember volunteering for things.

She: What about that horse foundation?

He: That wasn't volunteering. That was part of our unit. *(Husband was mounted police for fourteen years)* I wasn't volunteering for that. In fact, I would try to get out of anything associated with that as far as I was concerned.

She: *(Muttering)* Oh nice, okay, so this is going in the wrong direction.

What have you done in your life that you look back at and see as having done something good for the community or another person?

He: I've gone out of my way to help people at work: giving them money, buying them stuff.

She: Can you be more specific?

He: I give homeless people money to buy things, I buy them food, and sometimes I turn my back on violations that I could have arrested people for.

She: And that's a good thing?

He: I think so.

She: circumstantially?

He: Yes.

She: In what ways do you think you do good for the world, and what would you consider doing after you retire?

He: I don't plan on doing anything after I retire.

She: You sound like a total Dink in this interview.

He: Well, that's the way it is. I've done all the things I've wanted to do.

She: Do you see your role as a mentor to my boys?

He: Yeah, I suppose. In a way. I try not to cuss or yell at them or do things that are inappropriate around them.

She: In what ways do you think that you can help them to be good people?

He: By setting a good example in my behavior and how I treat people and them.

She: Do you remember what you said about them in your wedding vows?

He: I don't remember.

She: "I will teach your children to live with..."

He: Oh, honor...

She: And...

He: Integrity.

She: Courage?

He: Yeah, courage.

Both: *(Laughing)*

He: I don't know, sh*t. It's like you expect me to remember everything that I say.

She: You're the one that said it.

He: That doesn't mean that I remember everything that I said. That was like frickin' forever ago.

She: *(Still laughing)* That was not forever ago. It was like a year and a half ago.

He: I don't know.

I'm not sure where the urge comes from to help other people, but I wish more people felt it. While I'm certainly not applying for sainthood, I do seek out opportunities to give back to my community and to help others. Part of the reason for writing this self-help book series is to help others on a larger scale, but when I can help others locally and see the difference I'm making in real time, there's nothing more fulfilling.

In the year after I got divorced, I started a baking charity. There was an urge to do something and energy to be channeled, and I ran right at that idea. Stress baking is something I love to do because it's multipurpose: it gives me something to do while also being something I can make others happy with. My volunteer bakers and I would do a monthly surprise delivery to a service organization, and I always encouraged my volunteers to try to make it to at least one delivery. Deliveries were during the work day, but the looks on people's faces who worked at these sometimes thankless jobs made it all worth it.

Ironically, as I try to help more people by writing this book series, I have stopped stress baking and sending cookies and treats to work with my hubby at the police department. One day he called me with, "The bosses want to know if you're mad at them," he started. "Why would they think that?" I asked with confusion. "They think that's why you stopped sending treats," he explained. "DID YOU TELL THEM THAT I'M BUSY WRITING SELF-HELP BOOKS!?" I said as I made a "Really?!" face into the phone. Well, I felt bad, so I scheduled a three-day custom cut-out cookie-making weekend and sent shield cookies that were iced black with a thin blue line because I still wanted to show them that what they do is appreciated, even if it's not anywhere near the city I live in.

That feeling, the literal warming of your heart when you give back, it's addictive. Helping others is a feeling that cannot be described. It needs to be experienced. Find something you're passionate about and try to do some good with it. Even a plate of homemade cookies can be the light in someone's day that permeates to the people in their life. It only takes one act of kindness to change someone's world, and it will change yours too.

Chapter 16:

Happiness Is a Choice

SHE SAID

Why do there seem to be so many unhappy people in the world? Could there really be that big of a shortage of things to be happy about? And why do people who seem to have everything sometimes seem to be the most unhappy? A quandary that I will solve for you now…

The answers aren't overly complicated, but coming by the solution is not easy. In the many, many discussions with my husband about happiness in relationships, he always tells me that "Happiness is a choice." "Is it though?" I retort with sarcasm. As much as I do like to be right, he is pretty on the nose with his simplistic perspective.

Why aren't most people happy? They aren't focusing on the positive things in their lives. They are focusing on the things they don't have and that they can't change, which makes them eternally unsatisfied and grumpy. If the only thing in life that we can control is our reaction to things, then if we choose not to react negatively, we are essentially choosing to be happy.

Part of me feels like the more trauma or difficult situations that you've experienced, the more likely you are to be thankful that you aren't in those situations anymore. If you have something extreme to compare your current circumstances against, then maybe it's easier to be happy with whatever situation you are in as long as it's not as bad as the worst one you've experienced, right?

What about the people who haven't experienced extreme hardships or horrible relationships? How can they find happiness in their lives if they've never suffered? The good news is that you don't need to enroll yourself in boot camp to be jolted into choosing to be happy. Being happy is a mindset.

I find myself often in conversations with peers about how unhappy they find themselves in their relationships, and it always leaves me very thankful for the unconditional, nonjudgmental love that my husband so unselfishly provides me all day, every day. Oh sure, there are things that he does that bug the crap out of me, but I'm thankful for the reminders of how good I have it because it helps refocus my thinking in the happiness direction.

> *"Jane, I think I might need to start looking for a new job," Sandy said with a sigh of frustration as she walked into Jane's office.*
>
> *"Why? Won't you miss me?" asked Jane with a playful reply.*
>
> *"I don't feel like I make enough here, and they don't seem to pay more if you have more education," explained Sandy.*

"But are you really looking at the big picture? We get a lot of holidays off, and your job is pretty flexible with your kids. Not to mention the great coworkers we have. Would you really want to give all that up for more money?" asked Jane.

"I don't know. I mean, Leslie left for a dollar or two more an hour, and she hates it at her new job. She said her coworkers are mean, and her boss is a flake." Sandy said with a pensive pause.

"Sandy, there's more to a job than just the pay. I don't make as much as I'm worth here either, but the flexibility with my family is invaluable, and the job itself, I do love. I've made the decision to stay here and to be happy for the positive things I see in this place and this job," reasoned Jane. "You know I love you and want you to be happy, but I just want you to really think about what will make you happy with your life and your career," she continued.

"I hear you, but I don't know if I can get over how little I make for my level of education," Sandy replied.

"If you didn't know what anyone else in the office made, would you feel happier here?" asked Jane.

"I don't know. That's a good question," Sandy replied now unsure of her next steps.

"Sandy, why don't you take the weekend to think about it and talk with Alan. Maybe you'll change your mind, and maybe you won't, but at least you'll have taken the time to understand what you really need to be happy."

Sandy paused for a moment and said, "Okay, I think that's a good idea. Thanks!"

Monday morning, as the two sat together catching up, Sandy started, "I gave what you said a lot of thought, and you're right. I love it here too, and I think I can make the pay work if I just make some adjustments to my spending. Thanks for being my friend." "Sandy, you know I always want what's best for you," Jane said as they both bolted for the donuts whose arrival in the office had just been announced.

We spend a third of our lives at work, but that's just one place where we can choose to find happiness. The rest of our lives are relationships, and probably sleep, and probably going to the bathroom, but if happiness is a choice, why wouldn't we choose to be happy? I mean, doesn't it take more muscles to frown than it does to smile? Happiness should be easy, but sometimes it's not. The way to find more happiness is by changing how you think and see situations.

If you can retrain your brain to find the positives in the negatives, you will find it easier and easier to choose happiness. When your partner is annoying you, think about something they did that made you happy or a quality they have that endears them to you. When you get down about a job that you once were happy to have gotten, think about what you love about it. Is it fulfilling, do you love your coworkers, are there always free donuts? In every dark place, there exists a light switch. If you can find that switch in the darkness and turn it on, you'll see that there are a lot of reasons in your life to be happy.

HE SAID

She: On average, how would you rate your overall happiness with your life from 1-10?

He: Ten.

She: Why are you so...

He: No, actually nine.

She: Nine?!

He: There are deer outside.

She: Focus! Why are you so happy?

He: Because I have peace in my life.

She: What makes you happy?

He: My wife, and my family, and the fact that my job's almost over with.

She: Okay. Why do you always say that happiness is a choice?

He: Because it's easy to not be happy if you're focusing on the wrong things. If you're not worried about competing with anybody about material items, then it's easy to be happy. However, you have to choose to be happy because there are a lot of things that can drag you down. When you make the choice not to let those things affect you, you'll be a lot happier.

She: How are you able to be happy when things go wrong: like your battery dying on your car or like when your bank accounts got cleaned out by some rando thief?

He: Because none of those things affect the core things I value to be happy. The people who are important to me are still around, and if you have life and health, you should be happy that you have that. Little things don't matter in the grand scheme of things.

She: Why do you think that many people seem like they're never happy?

He: Because they're looking for the wrong things to make them happy. I think that when you compare yourself to others, you'll never be happy. You have to have a picture of happiness that is specific to you.

She: Do you think that people who haven't endured extreme hardships can choose happiness?

He: Being unhappy gives you perspective and gives you a clear understanding of the difference. It's easier to be happy after you've crawled through the trenches and come out than if you haven't.

She: What advice would you give to people on how to choose to be happy?

He: Just find out what's really important to you and set your life up around that. In my eyes, it's mainly peace. If you can find peace in your life, that's the best start. When there's peace in your life, then you can battle things that come along with more...

She: When you say peace, do you mean a stable home situation?

He: Yes, but stable in general. Your mindset needs to be stable and not overwhelmed.

She: Because it's not outside stressors adding onto stress you have at home?

He: Yeah. I've always had drama in my life until these last five to six years with you.

See, I told you the answer was simple, but choosing to keep life in perspective amidst the daily bumps in the road is not easy. Unfortunately and fortunately, I have not experienced hardships to the degree that my husband has, but I do recognize how very lucky and blessed I am in my circumstances.

You don't always need to stab yourself in the leg with a fork to be thankful that your leg doesn't hurt. Sometimes all it takes is a conversation with someone whose situation isn't as great as yours to help you realize how great you have it. Regardless of whether you come by happiness through hardship or happiness through a comparative perspective, the joy of happiness is still a choice that you will need to make every single day.

Chapter 17:

Live without Regrets

SHE SAID

Adulting and life can often be challenging and will try to pull you down, demotivate you, and make you unhappy. However, life is all about choices and how you choose to respond to the situations and opportunities that are laid out for you.

Think of life like the weather. It can stress you out even though you can't control it, and no matter the forecast, there will always be unpredictable changes for the better or worse. Sometimes you will be given a perfectly sunny day, but other times you will be caught off guard as an unpredictable downpour washes out your plans. It is up to you to decide whether to be a doer or a sayer when it comes to facing the challenges life presents you.

The doers are the people who set themselves up to be the most prepared as they can be to weather any storm. They make sure the seals around their windows are tight, check the roof for leaks, make repairs as they need to happen, watch the weather, pack an umbrella and sunscreen, and make sure their snowblowers are tuned up and full of gas because they value being prepared and planning ahead.

While they also understand that life is as unpredictable as the weather, the sayers will not find a way to push themselves to prepare for any kind of weather, good or bad. These people are often brought down even further when unexpected storms hit because they have not prepared and will not accept responsibility for their lack of preparedness. They complain about the leak in the roof when it rains but they do nothing about it, and they become stuck in the puddle of negativity and mediocrity.

Now is the time to analyze your life and your goals. Do you want to set yourself up the best way you can to weather any storm, or do you want to be left crying in the rain while standing next to a puddle that sprays muddy water on you with every car that passes by? Stop accepting that sopping-wet, miserable existence, and take charge of your life because you are the only one who can.

As you open your umbrella to ward off the rain, invite others to share the shelter of your ever-expanding umbrella. As your umbrella grows wider, the people that you have invited in will help support the edges as the rain falls harder and the wind picks up. Stop looking at other people's umbrellas with envy at the size, color, or designer label printed on the handle because while their umbrellas might be better in some aspect, those people may be the only ones standing beneath their shelters while trying to control them when it pours or when the wind turns them inside out.

Redirect your focus inward toward who is under your umbrella. Once you can do that, you will easily see the things that are the most important to you... the people who are standing there beside you, under your umbrella, and inside your heart.

Sucking less at life and adulting often means figuring out what works best for you, your own best practices for all aspects: money, stress, love, sex, friendships, everything. To grow in every area, however, you will need to push past the limits of your comfort zone and break through to achieve higher levels of success. On your climb upward out of the mire of mediocrity, bear in mind that happiness is a choice that you will need to make every day in every aspect of your life. Yes, some areas will be harder to find happiness in than others, but success without struggle is not rewarding or fulfilling and will not allow you to enjoy the gifts of humility and thankfulness.

Remember, the only person standing in the way of your dreams is you, so stop making excuses, put in the work, defy mediocrity, and live without regrets.

Bonus Chapter:

Suck Less at Sex

SHE SAID

There's a reason this chapter is hidden behind the proverbial red curtain so don't be looking for reasons to get offended. There's still time to walk away and still feel closure that you finished this book. There's not even a chapter number so really, it's okay to be finished; you won't hurt my feelings.

***

Sex. I said it. It's out there. If you think about it, none of us would be here to read this book and to be ashamed of the word sex if someone hadn't had sex to begin with. I'm just saying…

Whether or not the word makes you uncomfortable, the fact of the matter is that sex is an important part of life and relationships, and if you want it to get or be better, there needs to be a discussion about it. Sex and passion are what keep relationships exciting and away from roommate territory. I remember one afternoon when I was making Better Than Sex Cake for a dinner we were hosting, and my husband seemed very confused about the dessert's namesake.

Me: I'm making Better Than Sex Cake for dessert.

Hubby: That's not a thing. There's no dessert better than sex.

Me: Um, it's a super good dessert.

Hubby: Well, anyone who thinks that a dessert is better than sex obviously hasn't had good sex.

The physical relationship that my husband and I share has been electric from the very beginning, and it has stayed that way through our whole six years together. I just can't keep my hands off him.

But what is the secret to success in the bedroom, and what elevates "okay sex" to "great sex"?

Recently, I was enlightened to the fact that a few of my friends had been intimate with the same local tattoo artist, but they both raved about how great the sex was.

Me: What made it so great?

Friend 1: He was passionate and aggressive… he had sex like a Black guy.

Me: I don't know what that means.

Friend 1: That's how Black guys have sex… passionate and aggressive.

Me: I'll have to take your word for it. *(To the other friend)* Why do you say that he was the best sex you've had?

Friend 2: He made me feel attractive and wanted. He always wanted to hold hands, and he was a good cuddler too beyond just the sex.

Me: Hmm. What number rating would you give him on a scale of 1-10?

Friend 1: A high 9. Don't forget I was an escort for four years.

Friend 2: I hate your number systems, but if had to rate him, I'd say 10.

Me: This is the best morning ever. What else makes sex great though?

Friend 1: He lets you finish first.

Me: That's a must; I agree totally.

Friend 1: I like the passion and intimacy more than the penetration. The passion in the foreplay and the intimacy afterward… like the cuddling.

Me: Well, you're single now, maybe you should see if he's single and date him.

Friend 1: He was a walking red flag, but red flags are the best sex.

Some days, my life is so interesting, and that conversation was right up there with the one where one of my friends showed me her and her friends' sex score sheet… a running tally of names, number ratings, and reasons for the ratings. Fascinating stuff. Although, I did have to ask a lot of questions because these twenty-somethings sure have some weird acronyms and backward ways of explaining things in shorthand.

I must admit that I wouldn't have been able to touch on this chapter with any level of authority if it hadn't been for my amazing husband and the experience and expertise he brings to the relationship. On our last couples vacation, we were lying on an outdoor daybed watching the saxophone player entertain the after-sundown crowd. He was asking couples how long they had been together. When it came our turn, he asked Andrew who said, "Five and a half years," to which I shouted out, "And he's the love of my life!"

Quick on his feet like a good entertainer always is, the musician responded, "Tell me in one word what makes him the love of your life." I'm terrible under pressure, and the only thing I could spit out was "Patience!" Later that evening, Andrew said to me, "You should have said 'Cockateer'."

"Um, no one would have known what the heck that means," I responded. "Well, if anyone ever asks me that question again, I'll know how you want me to answer," I placated.

If you don't know what that word means (as most normal people wouldn't know), it means "Master of the cock. Almost jedi-like in skill". How do I know this definition? I Googled it the first time he said it because I accused him of making it up. "I did make it up. I started it," he said.

"No, you didn't!" Well, the entry in Urban Dictionary is dated 2006 so his story really could be true. I didn't realize I married a famous wordsmith.

Regardless of who etched the word Cockateer into a stone tablet and when, it is a fact that good, bad, or no sex can affect your mood, your relationship satisfaction level, and even your health so it's something you likely want to suck less at... or more of... or, well, now I'm flustered!

When I was writing the chapter on intimacy for my first book, *Suck Less at Love*, my oh-so-wise husband Andrew said, "Just tell everyone to sleep naked. That will improve everyone's intimacy." So wise. So articulate. So simple, but so true. Sleeping in your birthday suit is a very simple and easy way to increase or generate intimacy in your relationship, but while the solution is simple, getting there, not so much.

Sleeping in the buff requires a certain level of willing vulnerability that only happens when a relationship is healthy. I'm sure you'd never think, "He bugs the crap out of me, so I think I'll sleep naked next to him tonight." No, it's usually the exact opposite, "He is bugging the crap out of me so I'm going to wear the most full-coverage pajamas I own and sleep as far away from him as possible."

This simple intimacy hack only works if both parties are willing to sleep naked. "But my kids come into my bedroom," I've heard many times when I propose this idea. "You gotta stop that sh*t right now," I advise. "Are they dying every night to the point of needing to barge into your room?" I ask. Boundaries, people, boundaries. Healthy marriages produce better parents. Better, happier parents set great examples for children to know what healthy relationships should look like. Having a great sex life is key to having a healthy, happy relationship.

> *Jane loves Dick, but she's gotten bored of their sex life. It's always the same, it's practically on a schedule, and she finds herself less and less a willing participant. "I have a headache, Dick, and I've had a long day. Can we do it another time?" She heard herself say one night.*

"Oh. Okay," Dick said with a hint of concern. "Do you want me to get you some medicine for your headache?"

"No, I just need to go to sleep," Jane muttered.

The first time he was denied, Dick was understanding, but as the denials kept piling up with less and less sex in their marriage, Dick was starting to get frustrated and angry at his wife. The less and less sex they had, the harsher their tones got toward each other until Dick found himself sleeping regularly on the couch.

His lack of satisfaction was making him more irritable at work and at home, and his increasing unpleasantness was putting Jane off even more. The two grew farther and farther apart until Dick exploded. "Jane, I can't live like this without sex! What happened, and why don't you want to have sex with me anymore?" he interrogated.

"Dick, I don't see what the big deal is. It's just sex," Jane countered.

"It may not be important to you, but it's extremely important to me!" Dick continued. "Can't you feel like something's off in our marriage?" he asked as he stepped closer and softened his voice.

"Yeah, I can. I don't know... I think it's not as exciting as it used to be." Jane confessed as her eyes avoided his.

"Oh," Dick replied. Silence. "Well, I don't know what to do with that information," he said finally, breaking the awkward silence. A week passed of more awkward interactions, more avoidance, and more sleeping apart. One evening when Joy had gone to her best friend Poppy's for a sleepover, and Jane was doing the dishes, Dick came up behind her and initiated intimacy in a way he hadn't done before and with the passion and spontaneity they had enjoyed when they first met.

Forty-five sweaty minutes later, as they cuddled Jane said, "Wow, Dick. I'll take more of whatever that was." After a weekend of reconnecting again, they started to feel closer, happier, and less stressed. Jane realized that she needed to be more of a willing partner, and Dick realized that he needed to change things up occasionally.

The more great sex you have, the more sex you will crave. Think of sex like dining at a restaurant. You eat the same meal at the same restaurant once a week. However, over time, the go-to meal that you were once excited about starts to become bland and boring to the degree that you'd almost rather cook at home than go out. The grade of steak seems to be getting worse, the baked potato on the side isn't cooked through, and the vegetables are overcooked. Even the presentation is lacking. While the food is doing its job of filling your stomach, it isn't something to go out of your way for.

Now imagine that a new restaurant opens that is offering the same food as a special. That restaurant serves you the most mouth-watering, succulent appetizers before dinner, the steak is cooked to perfection, the potatoes are loaded and creamy, and the vegetables are crisp and hot. Dessert is even included after the dinner, and It. Is. Better Than Sex Cake Decadent.

Every time you visit the new restaurant, the special menu changes and is always a pleasant surprise. Now that you've enjoyed the very best meal, that's all you crave. You never want to go back to the first mediocre restaurant without the included appetizers and dessert. Why would you? You're addicted, and there's no going back. The standard has been elevated.

Great sex, like a great meal, means enjoying the whole experience. The leadup, or foreplay, can start outside the bedroom in flirtatious exchanges and can be drawn out with the physical. The longer the leadup, the hotter the action will be. The level of excitement, the passion, and the spontaneous modifications during the act are key to keeping the momentum up and both parties engaged. Afterward, the intimacy and cuddling, or "post care", are important to making sure that the overall experience isn't tainted by misconstrued intentions of just the physical act.

Now, who wants to go out for a steak? I know I do.

HE SAID

She: How important is sex to you in your relationships?

He: It's not important at all. I don't like sex.

She: Okay, this is serious. We have a lot of material to cover.

He: *(Pauses)* What do you mean, how important is it in a relationship?

She: This is for the chapter about sex.

He: We already had a relationship book.

She: *(Annoyed)* This is about JUST sex. Would you just answer the question! We are going to be here all day!

He: Like good sex or just regular sex?

She: I haven't gotten that far yet.

He: I like sex. That's all I can say is that I like sex.

She: UGH! Is there such a thing as bad sex?

He: No, some is just better than others.

She: What do you think makes sex great?

He: Me.

She: I'm serious.

He: Seriously. The thing that makes sex great is being able to adapt in the moment and being able to change things up and to be highly sensitive physically while being able to ignite emotions in your partner that gives the feeling of being in love and...

She: Well, does that mean you can't have great sex with a one-night stand?

He: No, not at all.

She: Well, then you're not defining it correctly.

He: What makes good sex is the ability to make your partner comfortable and to make them feel like they're being worshipped. You need to trigger an emotional response...

She: So, it's something that you do for them that they then reciprocate back to you? That sounds kind of one-sided.

He: It is one-sided. If I'm getting what I want which is sex, what can I do to get that other person to get into it and let themselves go... make them more open to being flexible with their boundaries... pushing them up against their boundaries and making them go past them. Willingly. Those are all good things.

She: Okay, so that's essentially you saying that if you make the other person feel comfortable, then they will open up more and allow you to do more things that will make you happy, right?

He: Yeah. Then it's not as boring.

She: Well, could sex be boring if it's someone you've only had sex with once? Is that even an option?

He: Yeah, but I think sometimes when you're having sex with somebody, you can kind of tell where it's going to go in how they respond to you. Not that I've ever had sex with anyone but my wife, but…

She: PHHHHH! Get serious. What do women think makes sex great?

He: Well, how would I know that? I'm not a woman.

She: Because you're supposed to know because of your experience. What made women want to come back to you for sex after a breakup?

He: The things I said. Making them feel comfortable and not ashamed and keeping them motivated and performing at a level that is better than they've experienced before. The more successes you've had with doing that, the more you know what's going to happen so that confidence is what women like.

She: Confidence in the bedroom.

He: Yeah. I've heard women say that there are men who don't seem to know what they're doing.

She: *(Giggling)* That probably happens a lot, actually.

He: I would think so.

She: So, how can people who have been together a long time make sex great?

He: There are a lot of things that would have to go into it like attractiveness. You also have to introduce novelty…

She: I thought you said you don't like costumes.

He: I've never been in that position where it's boring.

She: Because you haven't been with somebody that long.

He: You can try to use the aggressive man energy that worked in the beginning of the relationship, but if you have long-term issues that cause disdain by the woman, then it becomes harder and more work to get her in the mood. I don't think the magnetism that works for me works the same the longer you're in a relationship.

She: Even if there aren't any serious issues, if someone's been married for twenty-plus years…

He: Then there are issues. If it's boring, there are issues.

She: What if it's just boring because they don't know how to do it any differently and are just into a boring routine?

He: I don't do that. Do I do that?

She: We haven't been together for twenty-plus years.

He: Yeah, but I still don't do that. It's different every time, right?

She: Well, yeah…. That leads to my other question. How are you able to change it up every time?

He: Because I'm constantly thinking about it and envisioning things…

She: Like during the workday?

He: All the time. You need to be adaptive in the moment. Seeing different things and thinking, "This would be kinda cool"…

She: Like this morning?

He: It's like when you're dancing or are in a fight. You are always looking for openings.

She: Oohhhhh….

He: When you see those openings come up, that's where you can make changes. That's where a lot of guys mess up because they're focused on the feeling of it… and that's why some are premature and hyper-focused on the wrong thing. But when you are planning it all out, assessing it from many angles, and looking for those openings while playing the chess game several moves ahead, that's when it becomes more of a mindset that makes you able to become a true Cockateer.

She: Oh, for God's sake. So, what advice would you give people to improve their sex lives or suck less at sex for men and for women individually?

He: Communication and novelty. You need to have some kind of novelty and maintain some kind of attraction.

She: So, women need to stay attractive, and men need to bring the novelty?

He: Not necessarily. Both parties can do both, but there needs to be some intensity built up there so when you're going to do it, you're going to do it right. I'm not a big proponent of quickies. I think that's bull crap.

She: Really?!

He: I don't think that's a thing. When you're going to go into it, you want to be fully invested and put effort into it. To me, it's like an art, and I take it seriously. It's something that I want to do right, or I won't do it.

She: So, if I was like, "Hey, we got 10 minutes, do you want a quickie?" You wouldn't…

He: No, I don't want to do that. That's not something I'm into.

She: Huh.

He: It's not enjoyable.

She: Okay. Is there anything you want to say to people about sucking less at sex before I move on?

He: No, I didn't even want to say that.

Good sex can help your mental health, and your bond with your partner, and it's just fun! However, attraction is a big part of being able to have and maintain great sex. Attraction = passion, and passion = great sex.

The caveat to attraction is that it can only be recognized in a healthy relationship. In healthy relationships, men find their partners to be the most beautiful women they've seen because they love them, and most women who adore their men see them as superheroes. I know for a fact that I see my husband with a powerful stance and a cape blowing in the wind… just a cape.

Becoming a legend in the bedroom of your relationship isn't impossible and shouldn't be ignored because you would both be missing out on something that could elevate your lives in the greatest of ways. Figure out what you need, and what you can do to change it up, and enjoy each other. Life's too short to settle for bad sex.

Bibliography

Must-Know Rules for Converting Your 401(k) to a Roth IRA
https://www.investopedia.com/articles/retirement/08/convert-401(k)-roth.asp

Duluthian November—December 2022 Profiles in Leadership
http://duluthianmagazine.com/novemberdecember22/index.html

Cyndi Lewis was born in South Korea, was adopted to Wisconsin, and currently lives in Duluth, MN. Her decades of writing marketing copy, blogs, press releases, magazine articles, and short stories have sharpened her writing skills. Lewis is passionate about advising on subject matters that she is successful in and conveying advice in an informal, conversational tone.

Lewis wanted to challenge herself to release 3 books in 2024: The Suck Less Series, a 3-book self-help memoir-based trilogy that is funny, relatable, and snarky.

Book #1: Suck Less at Love: She Said, He Said Advice on Relationships

Book #2: Suck Less at Parenting: How NOT to Raise Little Monsters

Book #3: Suck Less at Life: Defy Mediocrity, & Live without Regrets

For updates, follow Cyndi on Instagram: @CyndiLewisAuthor, her author profile on Amazon, or www.CyndiLewisAuthor.com

www.ingramcontent.com/pod-product-compliance
Lightning Source LLC
Chambersburg PA
CBHW070459120526
44590CB00013B/698